The Broken ROAD

Healing after Divorce

Candy Block

The Broken Road: Healing after Divorce

Published by 5 Fold Media, LLC
www.5foldmedia.com

All additional emphasis in Scripture quotations are author's own.

ISBN: 978-1-942056-34-8

Library of Congress Control Number: 2016959325

To the Father and our Lord Jesus Christ. I thank You for saving me, for healing me, and for loving me.

To my wonderful parents for being there for me during my darkest hours. I love you guys more than you know.

To my best friend Missy for sticking by me.

And finally, to the most special dog there ever was and my special companion. You were always there when no one else could be. I praise the Lord that He brought you into my life.

Contents

Foreword

Foreword

In *The Broken Road*, Candy Block shares her personal journey of divorce recovery. Divorce is a road littered with booby traps and pitfalls as a cacophony of damaged emotions wreak havoc in the life of an individual. Divorced individuals have to struggle with rejection, abandonment, unforgiveness, bitterness, and anger, to name a few. Without intervention, the end result is depression, hopelessness, despair, and the death of joy. Many feel as though they have been plunged into a dark hole from which it appears there is no escape.

At the Healing Rooms of Greater Syracuse (member, International Association of Healing Rooms), we have ministered to many who have faced devastating circumstances in their lives. Whether it was devastating illness, the emotional trauma of divorce, damage due to loss, or a myriad of other challenges, there is hope in Jesus and there is hope for your future.

In this book, Candy courageously shares her intimate journey on the road to recovery. It will be of great value to anyone struggling with the reality of divorce. Divorce does not have to end in destruction—it can be a launching point to a greater future as negative emotions are overcome. Yes, divorce is a major changing point in anyone's life, but it does not have to permanently change their life expression. If we can learn to view life as a collection of seasons, as Candy has done, there is light at the end of the tunnel.

In *A Tale of Two Cities*, Charles Dickens penned these words: "It was the best of times, it was the worst of times." We all experience seasons in our life. We can go through glorious summer moments when the sun is warm, the sound of children playing can be heard, and it feels wonderful to be surrounded by the beauty of nature. But then winter comes, and the warmth of summer is quickly forgotten in the cold, harsh north wind.

That's how life is. Sometimes we are on the mountain, and other times we are in the valley. Sometimes we are rejoicing in the beauty of summer, and at other times we are despairing in the cold, harsh reality of winter. Life is a collection of seasons. Sometimes it is the best of times, but sometimes it is the worst of times. But no winter lasts forever.

Do not lose hope; do not despair! Whatever the trial in your life and whatever the cause, God is a good God. He is the provision and answer for whatever you are going through. God has an answer that can overcome any trial in your life as you seek Him in faith and follow His path to healing and restoration. Determine right now that you are not going to give up, that you are going to actively wait in faith, and that you are going to let God remove the stumbling blocks between you and your restoration.

Don't let the enemy steal your joy by convincing you it's not His will to restore you. It is His will. God does not want you to suffer, although while you wait for the fulfillment of His promise, He will use the wintertime in your life for good—if you know and love the Lord.

No winter lasts forever! As you work through this book and are openly honest with God, your restoration can come. Be encouraged. Winter is always followed by Spring! *Never give up!*

Study Candy's journey as laid out in this testimony of recovery from a devastating divorce, and be encouraged. The best is yet ahead.

Let the journey begin!

Vincent Aquilino

Director, The Healing Rooms of Greater Syracuse, NYS, and New England

Preface

Preface

Shock, numbness, disbelief, physical and emotional stress, anger, despair, and fear—these are the ways our bodies process grief. If you are experiencing any of these feelings due to divorce or any type of loss, don't worry, you are not crazy. This gamut of emotions is perfectly normal.

Grief can thrust a person into a realm of darkness that is unimaginable. It makes us feel like we are sinking ever so slowly to a deep and seemingly bottomless chasm of emotions. Why is this realm of human life so painful? The one true God made us to love and be loved. We need to be connected with people. The deeper the bond is, the greater the pain.

We all make plans for our lives. When they get derailed our world gets turned upside down. We strive so hard to make our life a never-ending story filled with sunshine and rainbows. We never give any thought to a storm rolling into our island paradise. Consequently, we are thrown into a vortex of emotions. This is why divorce is so painful. I was completely devastated when my ex-husband left me for another woman. My life was like broken glass that I couldn't put back together. The "happily ever after" had ended.

We may not know each other, and you might ask yourself the question, "Why would I even care about your story?" I don't know, but God has a purpose for His will. I may not be a Bible teacher or a minister, but my qualifications are the classroom of life, with Jesus as my teacher. What makes my story different from everyone else's? It is not any different.

The Broken Road

The truth is everyone goes through painful experiences. The most important factor is how you handle your grief. Regardless of the circumstance, pain is pain—and it can shake us to our very core and bring us to our knees. It can destroy the life we are accustomed to. My story could be the instrument to help you through your pain. It might help you see the light at the end of the tunnel and enable you to see how God can save you and help you through your own heartache.

Chapter 1

The Encounter

Chapter 1

The Encounter

It all started in the summer of 1995 when I was employed at a local department store. I was working in the cash office as the supervisor. One day, I looked up in surprise to find this smug-looking guy gazing at me. He was leaning on the counter like he was some ladies' man. I was kind of taken aback.

"Oh hi! Can I help you?"

"Hey, do you want to get married?" he asked, full of himself.

"Someday, but not to you," I quickly retorted.

Chuckling he said, "Oookay."

My first thought was, *Who does this guy think he is? I don't know him. He definitely is not my type. This man is wearing jeans and a black tee-shirt that says Rose's Bar. He's wearing an earring in his left ear. He has a goatee and mustache, and he is sporting a tattoo of a star on his right arm. My mother would kill me. The first words out of her mouth would be, "Oh no! I don't think so."*

Maybe it was a joke. However, little did I know that this encounter would change the direction of my life. He continued his inquest.

"So what's your name?"

"Candy. What's yours?"

"Eric."

Then there was a moment of awkward silence followed by another question.

"How old are you?"

"Boy you ask a lot of questions," I countered, thinking to myself, *What is this guy up to? Is he some sort of stalker? Does he think he is some Don Juan? That is all I need.* I prayed silently, *God help me.*

"Just wondering," he replied defensively.

"I'm twenty-six, if you must know." He looked at me like I was Pinocchio, and my nose was growing.

"No you aren't," he blurted out in disbelief.

"Yes I am."

"Prove it to me," he said.

I left the customer service counter for a moment to go get my driver's license. I was glad the store wasn't busy because I wouldn't have time for such games. I returned and shoved my driver's license in his face. "See," I said with a touch of snootiness.

Startled by my attitude, he took the license from me and examined it.

"I guess you are. You look awful young. I thought you were underage."

"I told you I was twenty-six," I said in a matter-of-fact manner. "Everyone thinks I look younger than what I am."

From that point on, Eric and I became friendlier with each other. He worked at the store too so while he was on break he'd come back to the customer service counter and talk or I would go back to the receiving dock and chit-chat with him. During one of our heart-to-hearts, he told me that he had broken up with his girlfriend a little while ago. He explained that he was still living with her because he had nowhere else to go. Looking back I can't imagine why I naïvely believed him. In the beginning I wasn't sure where this was headed or if I even wanted it to go anywhere.

My goodness, he was still living with his supposed ex-girlfriend! I was brought up Catholic and did have certain values and morals. However, I enjoyed the conversations and the attention. We had a lot of one-on-ones where he opened up and told me about his past and present situation. I took pleasure in the fact that he was opening up to me and trusted me with his burdens. My heart started going out to him.

Even during lunch breaks, we would drive to an empty spot in the mall parking lot and open up to each other. This went on for about a month without anyone becoming aware of our get-togethers. We had to be careful because his supposed ex-girlfriend's best friend worked at the store. Why was he trying to be secretive? I thought maybe he was waiting for the right moment, and our friendship speeded up the process of looking for a different place to live. I guess it's true that ignorance is bliss and love is blind.

I've since realized that the devil will use your weaknesses and desires to get you off track and move you outside of the will of God. I would wonder, *Was he still with her? Was I considered "the other woman"?* I didn't want anyone thinking I was a home wrecker. I wanted to believe everything he told me, and some of it turned out to be true. As a result of my own selfishness, I accepted everything as true. I wasn't a Christian yet, so couldn't I use the excuse that I didn't know any better?

God would eventually reveal to me the type of man he really was and would become. Before everything came to light, we did manage to have a couple of rendezvous outside of work. The first one was introducing Eric to my mother and my good friend. It was my day off, and my friend was up from New Jersey so she and I could go to the a big state fair. We were to catch up with Eric in the mall's parking lot. As we were driving through the parking lot, the image was a parent's worst nightmare. Eric was reclining on the hood of his car with his arms and legs crossed. He was wearing sunglasses and an Indian feather earring dangling from his left ear.

My mother said, “Over my dead body.”

I protested, “But Mom, you haven’t met him yet.”

“I don’t have to,” she shot back. “Look at him.”

I defended him, “You can’t judge a book by its cover. Just give him a chance, will you? I really like this guy.”

With an attitude she said, “Don’t expect me to like it.”

We agreed to meet at a local restaurant for some beverages and to get acquainted with each other. The little pow-wow carried on for about an hour. The conversation included everything from the mundane to my mother asking Eric a multitude of questions. Afterward, my mother seemed to soften a little bit.

The following day, before my friend and I went to the fair, we stopped at my workplace to see Eric. I bought him a pack of gum because he was trying to quit smoking. I was feeling like a school girl who was holding hands with a cute little boy. Finally I felt special. For the first time I felt wanted and needed. Everyone wants to feel desired and loved.

I have realized just because it feels good doesn’t mean that it is good or good for you. That is called deception. According to a Bible verse found in Jeremiah 17:9 (NKJV), “The heart is deceitful above all things, and desperately wicked; who can know it?”

I wasn’t trying to be deceitful; I wanted to do the right thing. Should I trust my own heart? Maybe to a point. The heart is complex and fragile. God knows our hearts and He searches them and gives to each of us according to our ways. Sometimes we have a difficult time seeing things in a straightforward manner. We get blinded by our fleshly desires and cannot see the truth in front of us. This is why we should pray and rely on God to show us the way. In this case, I didn’t.

One day the cat got out of the bag. During one of our lunch breaks, we were walking in the mall with my arm around his when we saw his ex-girlfriend's friend (the one who worked at the same store) in the food court. We kept walking and tried not to glance at her. We looked like the cat that ate the mouse.

"Uh oh, she saw us," I whispered to Eric.

"Just keep looking straight ahead," he replied.

Her mouth just about dropped to the floor. It was like "Extra! Extra! Read all about it! A scandal has just been uncovered."

I have learned from best-selling author and speaker Joyce Meyer that anything that you have to hide is not a good thing. I wanted to be the person who changed his life for the better. I wanted to be his redeemer (realizing now I couldn't—only God could) and be everything that he never had. Part of his problem, I thought, was he had the wrong people in his life. Maybe God put him in my path for a reason. This was my justification for being secretive. However, at this point I was unaware of the ignorance of my own reasoning.

Soon after, everything did come to light. Eric made the decision to move out. He went to live with his niece-by-marriage for a while. Needless to say, her family was less than happy about the arrangements.

This allowed us the chance to see each other. I would drive up to his niece's house and have dinner (which she prepared). Afterward, we would play cards and talk. He and I also went for walks, car rides, and went out for dinner. When we weren't spending time with each other, we would talk on the phone.

We no longer had to hide in the shadow of our deceitfulness. Was my heart really deceiving me? In retrospect, I did not see it that way. I was rationalizing all my thoughts and feelings. God's Word warns us against doing things we think we can get away with. He declares, "Do not be deceived, God is not mocked; for whatever a man sows, that he will also reap. For he who sows to his flesh will of the flesh reap corruption, but he who sows to the Spirit will of the Spirit reap everlasting life" (Galatians 6:7-8 NKJV).

The Broken Road

Oftentimes, people start off with the best intentions, but regardless of their motives, it can result in the worst harm.

Time progressed, and it was already late October. I realized that we had grown closer than I expected. Unfortunately, Eric had to move out of his niece's house because she was divorcing her husband. He had nowhere to go on such short notice. After talking it over with Eric, I decided to ask my parents if he could live with us until he was able to find a place of his own. Surprisingly, they agreed. Until this day, I still don't understand why my mother even agreed with this arrangement or how this idea was even decided. If you only knew my mother, this decision would be hard to fathom knowing her beliefs and her Catholic upbringing. This was to be one of the many ingredients that would make up the recipe called my life.

Chapter 2

The Beginning

Chapter 2

The Beginning

All the ingredients that make up our life story are part of God's plan for our lives. We all have a past that has already been written. We might not like how it was written (affected by some of our choices God allowed us to make), but it is a special blueprint the heavenly Father designed for His purpose and will. However, our future is full of blank pages waiting to record our life's journey. We need to accept the past and look forward to new chapters being written with God as our co-author. Even though your story is still being written, be assured the ending will be great.

Not long after moving in with my parents and me, Eric proposed to me. The most romantic part is he proposed to me on Valentine's Day. Of course, I said yes! I couldn't believe I was actually going to get married. A few months after the engagement, we decided to buy a house together. I was so excited that my life was going to be complete. At least, so I thought. I later learned that I wouldn't be complete without Jesus Christ. "For in Christ lives all the fullness of God in a human body. So you also are complete through your union with Christ, who is the head over every ruler and authority" (Colossians 2:9-10 NLT).

When we have Christ, we have everything we need for salvation and for abundant, healthy, and righteous living. Few people are content with their lives, so they search other religions or cults because they want a life with more meaning and purpose. They want answers to their questions. I personally discovered that Jesus Christ is the only source of fulfillment and the remedy to all our problems.

Life seemed to be headed in the right direction for us. Things could only get better. There was love and hope in both of us. It was a new beginning and there was so much to look forward to. Our love was as fresh as the dew of the morning, and I knew our love would hold us together and be the shelter that could weather any storm. As long as we loved each other, we could get through anything. "[Let your] love be sincere (a real thing)" (Romans 12:9 AMPC). In other words, let love be authentic and not fake. Real genuine love does not run out at the first sign of trouble. Love-driven marriages can endure any hardships as long as both people are willing to work at it together. When we hold on and let Jesus take control, He'll make our marriage better than it was from the start.

Eric and I were actually engaged for five years before we got married. However, during those five years, we had our ups and downs. We went to counseling to see if it would help resolve some of our issues. It did help improve our relationship for a short period of time, but we fell back into the same old pattern. Of course, part of the obstacle was we both were not saved and were living together without being married.

Knowing what I know now, a relationship between a husband and wife will not be stable unless Jesus Christ is the center of that union. As stated in Psalms 127:1 (NKJV), "Unless the Lord builds the house, they labor in vain who build it." A marriage without Christ at the center can never experience the spiritual bond the Lord brings to relationships. A marriage between a husband and wife is more important than the companionship they seek. Many people enter this covenant with unrealistic expectations. People expect something magical to happen. But marriage needs that spiritual foundation for that wondrous journey to take place.

Looking back, I was one of those who expected a Cinderella fairytale. You dream about meeting a guy who sweeps you off of your feet and you live happily ever after. It's the type of romance that Hollywood portrays in movies and the ones we dream about. But such fairytale marriages do not exist. If you are expecting a fairytale marriage, you will end up being very disappointed. Unlike the world would have us believe, love is more of an action and a choice than a feeling. A perfect example of love in action is Jesus Christ dying for us on the cross. He hung on the tree for love. Love is not a feeling; it's an act of your will.

Eric and I finally got married in July of 2000. The big day was upon us, and I was happy and scared all at the same time. I don't know about you, but when I think of weddings I think of the song that talks about bells ringing, the sun shining, and the bride and groom belonging to each other, loving and cherishing each other until the end of time, never feeling lonely anymore. Let me tell you, the bells did not ring and the sun did not shine. The happiest day of a girl's life is supposed to be sunny and beautiful. The day of the wedding it just didn't rain, it *poured*, and it was very windy too. We didn't love each other until the end of time, and at times we both felt lonely. I am not sure, but as I look back I think God was trying to tell me something that day.

After the honeymoon, we both went back to the humdrum schedule of our ordinary lives. The first few years of the marriage seemed to be going well. We still fought, but at the time it didn't seem as bad as before the wedding. I felt getting married made everything better; it made the bond between us feel more secure. We didn't have the pressures of planning the wedding and moving our mobile home onto our own land all at the same time. Dealing with both events created undue pressure that put a strain on the relationship. That was all behind us; now we could start moving forward.

Although the relationship seemed to have improved, I realize now that all our problems were just concealed in the recesses of our minds and ignored. Eric and I never worked through them. When we got in a fight, we would yell and scream at each other, use unkind words, make accusations, and he would damage something in the house. We allowed bitterness to enter the marriage because it was not dealt with beforehand. If allowed to grow, this seed will have a major impact on the martial union. You'll lose the emotional, spiritual, and physical closeness you once had with your spouse. I would mediate on Ephesians 4:31 (NKJV), "Let all bitterness, wrath, anger, clamor, and evil speaking be put away from you, with all malice." We need to be intentional about resolving conflict, otherwise the weeds of bitterness will eventually choke out the love in your marriage.

We felt the next order of the matrimonial progression was to start trying to have a family. He and I tried having kids on our own for about three to five months, but were unsuccessful. We made the decision to go to the doctors and get evaluated. My husband went for his test and was informed that he was perfectly productive. I, on the other hand, went through numerous tests (some painful), and found out I was not effective enough to conceive on my own. After all the tests were done, my doctor revealed to me that I had endometriosis. Endometriosis is a chronic female condition in which the cells which line the uterus grow outside of the uterus in other areas, such as the ovaries, bowels, intestines, and bladder. The lining that has grown outside the uterus responds to your cycle. As a result, lesions develop and create scar tissue. The abnormal growth leads to pain, discomfort, and infertility.

I was in a state of disbelief. The news was a big blow to my self-esteem. Trying not to get depressed, I told myself there are options out there to help couples have children. After talking with my doctor, Eric and I made the decision to try artificial insemination. I went through fertility shots and blood tests for three to four months, but to no avail. The only two choices available were IVF (in vitro fertilization) or adoption. IVF wasn't an option because our insurance did not cover this course of action, and we were unable to pay the hefty $10,000.00 per cycle ourselves. Furthermore, adoption was not a possibility either because Eric did not want to adopt.

My self-worth went down to zero; I felt useless to my own husband. I felt I let him down because he wanted children of his own, and I couldn't give him any. The way we perceive our own value has a direct effect on our conduct. Human worth is not based on possessions, achievement, physical attractiveness, or the ability to have children. Instead, it is based on being made in God's image. "So God created man in His own image" (Genesis 1:27 NKJV). God does not make junk or mistakes. Keep in mind you are special to the heavenly Father! "But the very hairs of your head are all numbered. Do not fear therefore; you are of more value than many sparrows" (Luke 12:7 NKJV).

True happiness in life comes from gaining a proper perspective of yourself through God's eyes. As Psalms 139:14 (NKJV) claims, "For I am fearfully and wonderfully made."

Because we were unable to have children of our own and Eric didn't want to adopt, I thought we would focus on ourselves and our marriage. I was hoping that my inability to give him children didn't change his love for me. In retrospect, I feel that was the beginning of a slow fade of the marriage. People and relationships never fall apart in a day. It's a gradual progression of thoughts that enter our mind and the choices we make. Be careful if you think you can escape the repercussions of compromising decisions. We often realize too late that there is a price to pay for compromising. When we start deceiving ourselves with conceding thoughts, know the end will come. It will be a journey you will regret.

Whatever balance there was in the relationship, it began to shift. Therefore, in June of 2001, to fill the void of not having children, I made the decision to get him a dog. I couldn't believe I talked myself into getting one. I was obsessive-compulsive about cleanliness, but then I knew Eric loved dogs. I called the man where our friends got their puppy to check if any were still available. There was one left, but he was already taken. However, he informed me that if the people didn't pick him up by a certain time, he would be ours. While I waited, I prayed to God about my decision. I asked the Lord, "If you want me to have the dog, than let him still be there, and if not, he won't be there."

I called the guy back, and he told me the dog hadn't been picked up. Eagerly I replied that I'd pick him up as soon as possible. Eric was thrilled that we were going to have a dog. He went to the store to get pet supplies while I went to pick up our new addition. The guy's grandson told me his name was Hercules. We liked the name so we decided to keep it. I thought I was getting the dog for my husband, but God had other intentions. Hercules turned out to be the best companion anyone could have. The name Hercules refers to a hero with exceptional strength. I will tell you that my boy lived up to the meaning of his name. Through the grace of God, that wonderful dog gave me the courage to get through my storms.

Getting Hercules only made Eric happy for a very short period of time. He started spending money on things he wanted for hunting and other recreational fun. Whatever he bought, it only made him content for a short period of time. It was like a drug for him—after the high wore off, then the crash came. Due to Eric's inability to wait to get things he wanted, we experienced considerable financial distress. This only fueled the tension in our marriage. I'm not sure if he was trying to compensate for his unfulfilled boyhood or he just like spending money. Knowing him for as long as I had, I saw it as possibly an emotional compensation for the lack of a childhood he had while growing up.

Much of what we've been taught by this world is a complete lie. The fact is that we cannot find happiness in buying things. We must understand this and never fail to realize that true happiness is found by having a relationship with Jesus and connecting with those people whom we love. Real fulfillment comes through having shared experiences that we will cherish. First John 2:16 tells us, "For all that is in the world—the desires of the flesh and the desires of the eyes and pride of life—is not from the Father but is from the world." In Luke 12:15 Jesus declares, "Take care, and be on your guard against all covetousness, for one's life does not consist in the abundance of his possessions." We become truly wise once we start to comprehend the truth that everything in this world will pass away. No lasting spiritual value can be found in material items. They cannot buy you eternal life. Food for thought can be found in Matthew 16:26, "For what will it profit a man if he gains the whole world and forfeits his soul? Or what shall a man give in return for his soul?"

As time went on, the bond between us started to wear thin. His spending increased, and he seemed more angry and discontented. He blamed the deterioration of the marriage on me; he claimed that I was unwilling to change. The fights became worse and more intense. I started feeling helpless, so I said a novena to Saint Jude. It seemed to help for a period time, but everything began to unravel like a ball of string. I just couldn't figure out what was happening, but I now realize some of the issues.

First, I didn't have a relationship with Jesus. Second, I was praying to the "saints." I came to realize that there is only one mediator between us and God and that is Jesus Christ (see 1 Timothy 2:5). Third, I was trying to understand why it was happening and trying to figure how I could fix it on my own. I tell you one little secret: you can't. Solomon wrote in Proverbs 3:5-6 (NKJV), "Trust in the Lord with all your heart, and lean not on your *own* understanding; in all your ways acknowledge Him, and He shall direct your paths." We must trust God with every aspect of our lives and believe that He is able to do with it what He wills. Pray and seek the Lord's direction because God knows what is best for us. He is infinitely wiser when it comes to knowing what we need and helping us with our problems. As people, we hate giving up control; we think we know what is best for ourselves—but we don't! You must turn every aspect of your life to Christ. I encourage you to take that step! Believe me, you won't regret it!

Chapter 3

The Not So Fairytale

Chapter 3

The Not So Fairytale

Nothing happens in God's world by chance or by accident. It says in Ephesians 1:11 (AMPC), "In Him we also were made [God's] heritage (portion) and we obtained an inheritance; for we had been foreordained (chosen and appointed beforehand) in accordance with His purpose, Who works out everything in agreement with the counsel and design of His [own] will." Every purpose and event is under God's control. He is the ultimate source of all power, authority, and everything that exists. Even Satan has to ask God's permission before he can act.

No matter what aspect of your life is out of control, rest in the fact that Jesus is Lord and He can handle your problems. If He can handle the whole world, then He can take care of you. David wrote in Psalms 103:19 (NKJV), "The LORD has established His throne in heaven, and His kingdom rules over all." Focus on God as a compassionate caregiver and not just as the Judge and Lawgiver.

Even though it was a year and a half before my life fell in the abyss of chaos, the last part of 2005 was the beginning of the end of our marriage. It all started after I found a girl's number in his phone. You are probably thinking I should not have been snooping. You are probably right, but he was acting very distant from me.

While he was helping our friend fix his car, he asked me to get his phone. As I grabbed it, I felt compelled to check who he had been talking to. While scanning his contacts, I saw a girl's name I didn't recognize.

Then the wheels in my brain started to turn, and all these thoughts started flooding my mind. Without thinking, I decided to call the number. It rang, but no one picked up. After making the call, I brought him the phone, not thinking she would call back. A few minutes later she did and asked if he had given her a buzz. He knew it was me, and he told her no, it was his wife. After hanging up, he looked like a bull ready to charge at a matador. I asked him who this girl was. He said with intense anger it was a girl from work. He used the excuse that he had to call her for work purposes. He couldn't always get through to dispatch so he called her on her cell phone. To keep the peace with him and myself, I decided to accept his defense and believe him. From that point on, I became suspicious of everything he did or thought he was doing.

It was only for a few months in the summer of 2006 that our marriage seemed to be doing a little better. I think one of the main reasons was I finally got a job. I was unemployed for about six to seven months, which put some tension on the marriage. The other reason was he decided to trade his old motorcycle in for a new anniversary-edition motorcycle. I didn't want him to and told him that we couldn't afford it. He said we would use some of his worker's compensation money for the down payment. I tried to explain to him why we shouldn't. He got mad, threw a fit, and still got the motorcycle anyway. What he wanted, he got—regardless of the consequences.

Toward the end of the summer I found out he was talking to another girl. Periodically, I would go online to check the numbers he was calling throughout the day. I found another unfamiliar number. I called, but this time I used *69 so whoever it was couldn't trace the call. She actually answered the phone, but as soon as she answered, I hung up. I couldn't believe it. He called me while I was on my lunch break that day. Not too far into the conversation, I confronted him about who this girl was. Consequently, we got into an argument; again he told me it was a girl from work. He explained to me she was having problems at home and he was talking to her and helping her out. I told him that if this girl was having problems with her husband then she needed to go to a counselor or talk to another woman. But getting through to his brain was a wasted effort.

When you need someone to talk to regarding personal issues, I strongly advise you not to put confidence in opposite-sex relationships. It is very risky. If you look to opposite-sex friends, a certain level of attractiveness and intimacy could develop. As a result, feelings could intensify and both of you could give in to any impulses you are experiencing. As it reads in Romans 13:14 (AMPC), "But clothe yourself with the Lord Jesus Christ (the Messiah), and make no provision for [indulging] the flesh [put a stop to thinking about the evil cravings of your physical nature] to [gratify its] desires (lusts)." We must not give into our desires and avoid such situations that open the door to such sins. Intimate friendships with the same sex do not present any risk; they provide you with emotional stability and confidence.

I was driving myself crazy wondering what he was doing and who he was talking to. I ultimately became obsessed with checking his phone calls. I even monitored them from work. I was going through the calls when I knew my boss wasn't anywhere in sight. I would call and hang up to make sure it wasn't another girl. It was affecting the quality of my life. I was turning into a person I didn't like. I actually threatened one girl I called. I told her that if she didn't stop talking to my husband, I would contact her husband to inform him of their conversations. She agreed, and I noticed on the call records that they weren't talking. Then he found out what I did, and he got very upset. Of course, after the huge fight we had he continued talking to her. Although I felt at times that what I was doing was wrong, he thought everything he was doing was just fine.

He and I were constantly arguing. I was very unhappy and it was showing emotionally and physically. My stomach started to bother me, and I was constantly depressed. I didn't have that little sparkle in my eye I always was told I had. I wanted to try and resolve our issues, but he never wanted to talk. He blamed everything on me, claiming I was unwilling to change. I was so desperate to fix my marriage. I started crying out to God. I even called a popular Christian television show for prayer a couple times a week. Things were not getting any better; they were actually getting worse. The rope that held our marriage together was getting thinner and thinner.

Now he started talking to his hunting buddy's wife. I was trying to ignore it and act like it didn't bother me, but it was eating me up inside. He told me they were having problems. Eric was more concerned about what was going on in other people's homes than his own. As time went on, they started talking more and more. Her husband eventually left her for another woman. I couldn't figure out why he would be concerned about that and why she didn't seek other counsel.

What put the nail in the coffin of our marriage was when he decided to stay at her house for Thanksgiving of 2006. I couldn't believe it! I asked him why, and he told me he didn't want to drive down there in the morning and drive back in the afternoon for dinner and then drive back down for the afternoon hunt. Nothing I could've said or did would have changed his mind. I was speechless.

At that point in time, I couldn't believe he picked her over me. It felt like our life didn't matter anymore. He truly left the marriage before it was over. He was being dishonest with himself and to our marriage. According to Webster's dictionary, dishonesty is a "disposition to defraud, deceive, or betray."[1] It says in Proverbs 10:9, "He who walks in integrity walks securely, but he who perverts his ways will be found out." A person's dishonesty will be his shame. People might think they are being "real," but they will be known for who they truly are. I started peering through the looking glass and seeing an image of the person I married.

I continued monitoring his calls and noticed that they were talking more frequently and each call was lasting longer. I discovered in December of 2006 that they weren't talking just for a few minutes—they were talking for thirty minutes to an hour at a time or more every day. I confronted him, yet again, about these lengthy phone calls, but to no avail. They went right on with their frequent and long phone conversations. I put my feelings in the hiding place of my mind as best as I could. I didn't want anyone to know how it was affecting me.

The match that lit the fuse came when he wouldn't admit that what he was doing was cheating. At that point, I wasn't sure if it had reached

1. *Websters Collegiate Dictionary*, 1913 Edition, s.v., "dishonesty."

a physical level, but all the signs led to an emotional affair. An emotional affair is when a person invests more of their emotional energy outside the marriage, but also receives emotional support and companionship in a new relationship. Some people feel that it is not considered cheating because there is no sex involved. Don't be deceived. Emotional affairs are a gateway to sexual affairs. Anything that leads you outside the bonds of your marriage is cheating. Clearly stated in Hebrews 13:4 (NLT), Paul writes: "Give honor to marriage, and remain faithful to one another in marriage." This goes against what our morally degenerate culture promotes today. Don't be misled by the world. Believe God's Word. Couples need to keep their marriage happy and strong and pray for each other. You must remain faithful in mind and in body.

Eric was living in his own darkness, unable to see that he was cheating on me. I couldn't handle the deception any longer. I left him for a week in January of 2007. I packed some clothes and stayed at my parents' house. I couldn't believe how precarious my marriage had become. I was desperate to save it.

My mother was listening to a local Christian radio station and heard an advertisement for The Healing Rooms. It is an international ministry where people go and receive prayer for physical and emotional healing from born-again followers of Christ. She mentioned the place and suggested that we go and look into it. I met the most wonderful people there. I signed in, and they asked what I needed prayer for that day. I went into one of the prayer rooms and discussed my situation. The prayer team in the room, through Jesus Christ, ministered to me by means of Scripture and prayer. Afterward, I felt a sense of peace and hope.

I called my husband Friday morning to see if he was open to the idea of talking things out. I suggested to him I would buy pizza and wings. He was very hesitant and not really open to the idea. It was like I was begging him to accept my proposal. Was I so hopeless and desperate to reduce myself to groveling? Hearing a disheartened sigh, he agreed to the meeting. At that moment, an explosion of hope welled up inside of me. I convinced myself I was going to save this marriage and make it work. Even though I was praying to God to help restore what was lost,

I was trying to do it in my own strength. No one can! Jesus said in John 15:5 (NKJV), "I am the vine, you are the branches. He who abides in Me, and I in him, bears much fruit; for without Me you can do nothing." Christ is the root of the vine. The root supports the tree and supplies all the nutrients needed to survive. Without that root, the tree dies. If we are without Jesus Christ, our efforts will be fruitless.

After work that Friday, I placed the order for the pizza and wings and took the thirty-five minute journey home. I had plenty of time to pray and talk to God. I asked Him to help save this marriage. This man was the love of my life. At that point, we had been together for twelve years. I did not want what we had to be a wasteland of defeat. I didn't want to be part of a growing statistic. This sacred union was worth saving. I was pleading with God that my husband would feel the same way.

We both got to the house around the same time. He let Hercules out and before we ate I started expressing my thoughts and feelings to him. Having previously rehearsed the conversation, I was making everything my fault and I petitioned to him that I would change. I told him I wanted another chance. At first, he was not very receptive. He didn't think I would change. It was as if he agreed everything that happened was my fault. Then he agreed to give us another chance. Praise the Lord! I was on cloud nine! God had answered my prayer.

The subsequent couple of months appeared to have improved. After the so-called "reconciliation," he went and bought snowmobiles for the both of us. We spent a lot of our time on the weekends with our friends, snowmobiling and just hanging out. I thought things were really improving. I even checked the phone records to see if they were really talking to each other. I couldn't believe it! There were no phone calls between them. He truly wanted to work at the marriage. The first weekend of March we went to Atlantic City because his company was having an awards dinner. In separate cars, we went down with his hunting buddy and his girlfriend. Yup, that is right! That hunting buddy who left his wife—that wife my husband had been talking to. Talk about strange.

Candy Block

Not long after our little weekend trip, he slowly started acting removed from the relationship again. I couldn't figure out why. I was striving very hard to change and please him. The week after we got back from Atlantic City, I was let go at the bank. I was in a state of shock! Why did I lose another job? Then we started fighting, and everything I felt we accomplished began to unravel. I felt powerless. I was unable to make sense of what was happening. I've since realized that without Jesus in your life, nothing will make sense. "In this new life, it doesn't matter if you are a Jew or a Gentile, circumcised or uncircumcised, barbaric, uncivilized, slave, or free. Christ is all that matters, and he lives in all of us" (Colossians 3:11 NLT).

Jesus Christ is all in all; He is our hope and happiness. Through the help of our friend, I was able to get a job at a movie rental store. I especially liked the job. I was able to talk and interact with all types of people. One of the perks of the job was that you could watch free videos. I thought getting a job as quickly as I did would make him happy. Clearly it did not. The whole relationship was on a downward spiral through a black hole, never to be seen again. Every day was like walking through a landmine.

I became very suspicious again. I started monitoring his calls once more by looking in his phone and on the Internet. In addition, I was checking his wallet and his clothes. I was driving myself mad. The only reason I examined his clothes was there were a few times he came home late. Plus there was an incident where I locked my keys in the car, and I had to call him to come and unlock the door with his keys. He became furious and he began yelling at me. He voiced to me strongly that he was going to be late leaving work. I didn't understand why. He usually got done around three o'clock and went home. Without getting into sordid details, that day when I got home, I did discover some evidence. I could feel the anxiety wearing on me.

Everything erupted like a volcano on May 7, 2007. We had been arguing a few days prior, and he was treating me like the enemy. On account of the war going on between us, as soon as I left work that night I called the Christian television show I had been calling previously for prayer. Halfway home my connection cut out. I never received the prayer I desperately wanted. I couldn't believe the call was dropped. I knew it was a divine intervention from the Lord. Afterward, I had this strong feeling to check the middle console of his car. I pulled into the driveway and my stomach was in knots. He was already in bed because he had to get up early for work. I continued praying to God.

While I slowly and quietly opened the car door, my heart started racing like a racer going a hundred miles an hour. I lifted up the console lid, and lo and behold there was a cell phone. My heart started to sink into my chest. I turned the phone on to see what this phone was all about. I recognized some of the numbers. They were some of the girls he had been talking to in the beginning. Of course, there was hers—his hunting buddy's ex-wife. I even checked their text messages to each other. Until this day, there are some I vividly remember. For example, one read, "Key is in truck, back lot, room 309." She also sent him a picture of herself on some beach; it was entitled, "Here, this is to tide you over." Another one read, "I can't wait 24 hours to see you."

At that very moment, my heart sank further down and out of my chest. My life as I knew it came to a screeching halt. I thought to myself, *How could he do this to me, to us, and to the marriage?* I was devastated beyond comprehension. It was too late to call my parents so I called our friends. I told our friend everything I discovered. There wasn't much he could say or do other then try to console me. After talking with our friend, I had to make an effort to compose myself and act like the world didn't end. I took a shower and went to bed.

Of course, I couldn't sleep. While lying there, I kept praying and talking to God. I tried so desperately not to cry, but my eyes kept filling up with tears. How did the marriage get this far? How could it be saved? God was the only one who could save it. God told the Israelites through Isaiah 30:15 (AMPC), "For thus said the Lord God, the Holy One of Israel: In returning [to Me] and resting [in Me] you shall be saved; in quietness and in [trusting] confidence shall be your strength. But you would not." I didn't trust in the Lord, and I didn't have a true relationship with Him.

Salvation only comes from God. You must wait for him in quietness and trust. We should lay aside our endless effort and allow Him to act.

Chapter 4

The Culmination

Chapter 4

The Culmination

Why do we wait until we are in a category five hurricane to seek God? We hold off reaching out to Him because we think we can do things in our own strength. People intently pursue our merciful God only when they are in trouble. Some do not at all. We feel we are the only ones with the answers and know the solution to every problem. If this is the case, why is the world the way it is today? The Great I Am knows that if we didn't have any problems, we would not seek Him. As it is told in 2 Chronicles 20:2-3, King Jehoshaphat needed to hear from God because "a great multitude" was against him. As a result, he "proclaimed a fast throughout all Judah." I think we should seek God as though we are desperate all the time; maybe then we wouldn't have hurricane-sized trials.

We both laid there motionless. Still crying and praying to God, I was paralyzed with grief and unable to sleep. I was waiting for the moment I dreaded—Eric's alarm going off. The second it buzzed, my mind was racing with thoughts of how he would react to my taking the phone. He went about his normal routine of getting ready for work. I was desperately praying that he wouldn't notice the phone missing until he arrived at work. I acknowledged every movement he made. I heard him leave the house and lock the door, I heard him get in the car, I heard the car start, and then I heard him back out of the driveway. I continued praying.

Sorry to say that specific prayer was not answered. Sounding like a racecar closely reaching the finish line, he drove fast and furiously back into the driveway. I listened to the car door slam with tremendous force, and I immediately thought, "Here we go." Eric came exploding into the house. It was as if Mount St. Helens erupted again. He shouted as loud and enraged as he could, "Where is the phone?" Jumping out of bed like a jack-in-the-box, I began screaming and asking him about her and the phone. He was being evasive; he wouldn't answer any of my questions. He persisted in asking me what I did with the cell phone. I yelled right back and told him I broke it and threw it in the woods. His face became almost as red as lava. He threatened me and demanded I go get the phone. While his fury was stilling spewing, my poor Hercules laid quietly on the bed not understanding what was happening. Concerned at what point he would no longer control his reactions, I went and got the phone. Grudgingly, I flung the phone at him. Nothing else was said between us. Then he stormed off and slammed the door as he left.

I was left breathless. I started crying like never before. My little world had come crumbling down. As I lay back in bed, Hercules cuddled right up next to me. He could sense that I was very upset. Still to this day, I praise the Lord this wonderful dog was with me because he brought such comfort. The gears in my head were grinding. How could I have let this happen? I realize it was not completely my fault or totally his fault. We both had a part in the collapse of our marriage. He might have administered the final blow that killed our dreams, but I was an accomplice. In James 4:1-2 (NLT), James probes the root cause of division: "What is causing the quarrels and fights among you? Don't they come from the evil desires at war within you? You want what you don't have, so you scheme and kill to get it. You are jealous of what others have, but you can't get it, so you fight and wage war to take it away from them. Yet you don't have what you want because you don't ask God for it." The basic cause is evil desires battling within us; it is very destructive. James is telling us the source of these conflicts is to be found in our self-seeking determination to please ourselves. People will do whatever it takes to get what they want. Jesus said to deny yourself and take up your cross.

I had a strong urge to call and interrogate Eric's girlfriend about the phone and their relationship. I was tossing the idea back and forth in my mind like a game of ping pong. Should I call or not; should I call or not? It was pure insanity. I made the decision that I needed to talk to her. My hand was shaking with every button pressed. After she answered, I immediately confronted her on why she got my husband a phone. She replied by telling me it was due to the fact I was having a spasm about him talking with other people, including herself. I was told he had every right to talk to whomever he wanted. The women was so blinded, she couldn't comprehend what she did was wrong. I expressed how difficult it was to live with him. Blatantly, she suggested to me that I should leave him. Reflecting back, I now realize why she told me to give up the ship. She wanted Eric all to herself. Of course, the conversation did not lead anywhere. After the banter, I remained in bed playing the soap opera over and over. All it did was make the anguish worse.

The next two days were like living in the aftermath of war. Destruction had been completely accomplished. Not one word was spoken between us. He didn't want to talk or discuss the situation. I felt non-existent. On Wednesday, May 9th, I finally confronted him to see if we could resolve the battle waging between us. There were no peace talks. He simply told me that he couldn't take it anymore. He made the decision to pack some clothes and go stay with our friends for a while to think things through. I strongly feel he had decided to leave long before the war climaxed. All that was left was Hercules and me and a pile of shattered memories and unfilled dreams.

My parents were in a state of shock. They couldn't believe my own husband would treat me like garbage and throw our life away. My mother suggested the Healing Rooms again. In desperation, I decided to go back. The only thing I wanted prayer for was the salvation of my marriage. Amazingly, this catastrophic event lead to the salvation of my soul. I was one of the ones crying out to God due to a life-altering event. I started going for prayer every week. These people were so anointed, and you could strongly feel the presence of the Holy Spirt. Surely God would answer my prayers; He would save the marriage.

The Broken Road

Over the next few weeks and months we hardly talked. Once in a while, I would call or visit him to see if he wanted to try resolving our chaotic mess. He wanted nothing to do with it. He was more interested in spending time with our friends then finding a resolution. He was making no effort at all. It was a one-sided effort; I felt like a fool. It was like trying to fill a balloon with a hole in it. Looking back, I can't fathom the fact I put myself through such humiliation and pain. I am certain that in his mind it was over. He already moved on in the direction he wanted to go. Without a doubt, he was still seeing her. I praise our Lord for my parents, Hercules, and a few friends who helped me through those rough times.

I continued seeking God, and it was the middle of the summer when I finally gave my life to Jesus Christ. I was watching a Christian TV program. It was at that point I decided to take that step of faith. I felt renewed and joyful. I was so convinced that God was going to save the marriage. Let me tell you, God's plan isn't always our plan. "Many are the plans in the mind of a man, but it is the purpose of the LORD that will stand" (Proverbs 19:21). God's purpose often thwarts our plans. We must remember that His ways are higher than ours, and His thoughts are higher than ours (see Isaiah 55:9). God is sovereign and His plan (the best plan) will be fulfilled in due time. The Healing Rooms gave me my first Bible. They suggested starting in the book of John. Little did I know that I was desperate and thirsty to know the one true living God and His Word. I was hoping by praying and getting into the Word, He would restore the vows we took. On the contrary, God restored me.

No matter what I was doing or where I was, I would replay the whole tragedy in my mind like a movie without an ending. This poem I wrote conveyed all the feelings I was coping with.

After all the battles fought and now the war over, I rest my case.
My soul is crushed. My heart is heavy.
The life we had left shattered in a million pieces on the floor.
I can't believe you were the one who left me standing
on a road I didn't plan.
Darkness pulls the strings.
There is nowhere to hide.

Candy Block

All I can see are broken memories.
Wounds that no one else will ever see.
Wounds that don't seem to heal.
My strength is almost gone. How can I carry on?
Pain so deep that I've lost my will to fight.
I want to believe there is meaning here.
After you left and walked away, there was nothing I could say.
So I cry out with all I have left.
Let me know the struggle ends.
I try to pick up the pieces that are broken.

Toward the end of the summer it looked like there was a glimmer of hope. During a few conversations Eric made it sound like he wanted to try and work things out. We even took a motorcycle ride to Lake George. In addition, we ended up buying him a new Nitro because he claimed he couldn't afford the gas in his truck and maintain his other car. At the end of the following week, he completely changed his mind. He only used me to get my cousin's husband's vehicle discount. I should have realized he wasn't interested in reconciliation. Every time I would try to discuss our issues, he would get defensive, irritated, and change the subject. His relationship with his hunting buddy's ex-wife was much more serious than expected. I still had not lost hope. God can restore anything dead, but He will not go against someone's free will.

I kept praying, getting deeper into the Word, and even started fasting. It was amazing how God was talking to me through His Word, songs, people, and just being still in His presence. It was bringing much-needed comfort. I was still having a hard time dealing with the trauma. There would be times when I would be taking a shower, and out of nowhere I would start sobbing hysterically. I didn't want to eat. At times I would just sit in my chair and stare into oblivion. I can vividly remember the sadness overshadowing my face. When I would cry, Hercules would come and put his head on my lap. Then when I hugged him, he would lick the tears streaming down my face.

The Broken Road

My husband left me to fend for myself. I took care of the house from repairs to mowing the lawn, snow blowing, and maintaining the finances. Eric completely detached himself from the marriage. By the grace of God, I landed a job with a small CPA firm. It enabled me to pay all the bills he left me to be responsible for. After his little trick of deception, leading me to believe he wanted to reconcile, he took his name off the joint bank account and terminated our phones. I started feeling overwhelmed. I was not going to give the devil a foothold. I kept proclaiming Philippians 4:13 (NKJV), "I can do all things through Christ who strengthens me." I wanted to rely on Christ's power so I could face all my circumstances with contentment.

I still wanted to put all the pieces of our life back together. I kept praying for God to give me a sign that it was over between us. One phone call revealed the decision that had to be made. He clearly had no desire. At one point in the conversation, I posed a question related to "her," and he told me he was friends with her and in a relationship with someone else. He definitely was not telling the truth. Only God knows why he lied. It wasn't until a few years later when he finally admitted that he had been in a relationship with her all along. God gave me the sign. It was time to concede this war and file for divorce. My whole world disintegrated. There were no pieces left to glue.

My pain was far from over. I cried out to Jesus so many times to deliver me from this humiliation and heartache. Each time I wanted to give up, Jesus gave me the strength just to keep breathing. Trying to be still before God, all these negative thoughts flooded my head like waves coming to shore. I was so afraid and tired of holding on. I did not want to be a failure. One of Satan's favorite weapons is fear. However, God was right beside me holding my hand and healing my heart. I had to claim Romans 8:28 (NKJV), "And we know that all things work together for good to those who love God, to those who are the called according to His purpose." The most important step I had to make was moving forward.

I started looking for lawyers. I found one I thought was going to "give it" to my husband good and make him pay for what he did. I proceeded to file the necessary paperwork and pay him a retainer along with a picture of my soon-to-be ex. I stood back and waited for the fireworks to begin. I was completely shocked when he did not call ranting and raving. Being curious, I called to see his reaction. He sounded pretty calm over the phone. He told me when he was served the papers, and he would be getting a lawyer. It felt like there was announcer yelling out: "Let the games begin."

I knew, with God's help, I had to come to terms with the end of my marriage. In the gloom of my weakness, I was still struggling to believe and accept the fact that he left me. I thought we would be together forever. Apparently, he didn't place much value in our marriage. It was very hard to accept. I did have biblical grounds. He cheated and did not want to stay with me. Even though I wasn't saved at the time, he was unfaithful. The biblical reasons made me feel less condemned. Once I accepted Jesus as Lord and Savior, everything was covered under the blood and I became new. Jesus was our ransom. He paid with the shedding of His blood. "In him we have redemption through his blood, the forgiveness of our trespasses, according to the riches of his grace" (Ephesians 1:7). I was truly forgiven and could look forward to a new future.

Through Jesus, I started a new life in Him. Like it says in 2 Corinthians 5:17 (NKJV*),* "Therefore, if anyone is in Christ, he is a new creation; old things have passed away; behold, all things have become new." God truly wanted me to have a fresh and renewed life. This new life requires a new way of looking at all people, a new way of thinking and reacting to the world and perseverance. If I continue my new life in Him, I will be completely free of strongholds and the enemy who wants to destroy me as long as I submit to God. I had to remember at the end of a story there is an ending, but in life, when there is an ending, there is a beginning.

Chapter 5

Why Is Not the Question

Chapter 5

Why Is Not the Question

The destruction of my marriage was the pivotal turning point in my life. It redefined my existence and purpose. However, the impending divorce was not the only incident that affected my life. I went through a three-year rebound relationship (which I will touch on later) and was unemployed for three and a half years.

All these trials occurred simultaneously within a four-year period. From time to time it felt as though I was going to have a meltdown. When we are in constant turmoil, we have to remember not to give in to our fears. Philippians 4:6-7 states, "Do not be anxious about anything, but in everything by prayer and supplication with thanksgiving let your requests be made known to God. And the peace of God, which surpasses all understanding, will guard your hearts and your minds in Christ Jesus." A good thing to remember is to turn your worries into prayers. When we worry or are unduly concerned, we do not trust God. If you start feeling anxious, start praying because it is an outlet for anxiety and an antidote for worry. You will experience peace that only He can give, not the world's (see John 14:27).

This may be hard to fathom, but you can have peace during your trials! All you have to do is release your faith. More importantly, you will not know how awesome God really is until you have been through a storm. You must realize that there is no such thing as an accident.

No human being likes going through adversity, but pain does have a purpose. You might not want to believe or accept it, but it is true. I felt the same way, but I look back and realize that my life is so much better than it was before. Think about it—if it weren't for trials, we'd take things for granted and become complacent. Sometimes we just need to be humbled. I realize it is uncomfortable and inconvenient, but after the storm passes look at the rainbow God created for you. The resulting growth is for your benefit, and you will be better off than you were before the upheaval. Just exercise your faith.

According to the dictionary, faith is "Firm belief, resting on probable evidence, in regard to important moral truth; reliance on testimony; belief."[2] Having faith in God (a God you cannot see) and His ability to take care of you in every aspect of your life does seem illogical. The writer of Hebrews states, "Now faith is the substance of things hoped for, the evidence of things not seen" (Hebrews 11:1 NKJV). We need to exercise confidence and assurance by acknowledging that even though we don't see Him working, God will help us and we will receive His promises.

We all go through tragic events. We have loved ones die, our spouse leaves us, we lose a job, or our health is not good. The outcome of our circumstances is dependent on how we handle them. If you have experienced a great loss, admit the feelings you're experiencing to Jesus. He knows and understands what you are going through. Don't hide your grief; Job didn't. The book of Job is a perfect example that demonstrates God's sovereignty and the meaning of faith. It also addresses the theme of "Why do the righteous suffer?" You are probably thinking, "What does that have to do with me?" We all suffer and need hope. Job's story was meant to teach us and to bring us encouragement. We might not understand why we suffer; however, the secret things belong to the Lord (see Deuteronomy 29:29). Sometimes we suffer as a consequence from a bad decision or action either from ourselves or another person. On occasion, it is an attack from Satan on our lives.

---

2. *Websters Collegiate Dictionary*, 1913 Edition, s.v., "faith."

Candy Block

The apostle Peter warned us in 1 Peter 5:8 (NKJV), "Be sober, be vigilant; because your adversary the devil walks about like a roaring lion, seeking whom he may devour." When you are feeling alone, weak, or helpless and find yourself focusing on your problems, those are the times when you are most vulnerable to Satan's attacks. And those are the times we need to seek strength and support from God and other believers. James instructed us how to be vigilant. "Therefore submit to God. Resist the devil and he will flee from you" (James 4:7 NKJV). Remember, the devil flees from God's children who wear the armor of God and resist him.

Job was considered a righteous man. God said, "There is none like him on the earth" (Job 1:8). He was counted blameless, but Job was not sinless. Satan falsely claimed that Job worshiped God because everything was going well, and his worship was not out of love but due to the fact God had given him so much (see Job 1:9). God permitted Satan to afflict Job, but he could not harm him (see Job 1:12). Everything happened to Job all at once. He lost his children, servants, livestock, herders, and his home. Yet he did not curse God. Instead, he tore his robe, shaved his head, and worshiped the true living God in spite of all that had befallen him. In Job 1:21 (NKJV) we see this patriarch declare, "Naked I came from my mother's womb, and naked shall I return there. The Lord gave, and the Lord has taken away; blessed be the name of the Lord." The devil did what he wanted; it actually proved Satan to be a liar and Job an honest man because Job continued worshiping Jehovah Rapha (the God who heals).

Satan went before God again. He believed Job was faithful because he was willing to accept the loss of his family and property as long as he wasn't physically harmed. "Then Satan answered the Lord and said, 'Skin for skin! All that a man has he will give for his life'" (Job 2:4). God agreed to allow Satan even more latitude by replying, "Behold, he is in your hand; only spare his life" (Job 2:6). Then the devil afflicted Job from the top of his head to the soles of his feet with painful sores. He humbled himself before God and then scraped himself with broken pottery and sat in ashes as a sign of mourning. Job's wife said to him,

"Do you still hold fast your integrity? Curse God and die" (Job 2:9). Not only did the devil torment him but tempted him by using his wife to tell him to curse God. Conversely, instead of caving in, Job relied on God's grace to hold him up. Job's faith didn't falter, and Satan's intentions against him were defeated.

Job was struggling emotionally, physically, and spiritually; he was in the pit of despair and had difficulty accepting his circumstances. He actually cursed the day he was born (see Job 3:4). Job's friends heard what happened to him, and they left their homes to go sympathize with him and comfort him (see Job 2:11). They wept and mourned with him for seven days and sat in silence out of respect. After Job broke his silence, he vented over his grief. He could find no meaning in his suffering. He professed that he lacked the inner resources to cope with his anguish.

His friends might be viewed as a third test. Their visit turned into a long theological debate over what caused Job's suffering. His friend Eliphaz expressed to Job his suffering must have been due to some sin in his life. He urged him to repent and seek God's favor. Bildad and Zophar agree Job must have committed some evil to offend God and his children brought their deaths on themselves. Zophar was the worst of them all. He went as far as to say Job deserved more punishment. Job continued asserting his blameless behavior and pondered man's relationship with God, even telling his friends they were of no use to him whatsoever (see Job 13:4).

Job becomes impatient and laments the injustice of God. He wants to complain to God but cannot physically find Him. Then another friend, Elihu, puts his two cents in and tells Job that he has spent too much energy vindicating himself rather than God. Elihu also believes Job must be wicked to suffer like that, and his excessive moaning is an act of rebellion against the one true God.

To understand the debate amongst Job's friends concerning his suffering, you have to understand the times and culture during that period. He was living in an era when it was common to believe that suffering was understood as a punishment for certain behavior.

God finally has enough and answers Job in a storm and demands he be brave and respond to His questions, "Who is this that questions my wisdom with such ignorant words? Brace yourself like a man, because I have some questions for you, and you must answer them" (Job 38:2-3 NLT). God's questions were intended to show Job how little he knew about creation and how powerful God really is. The Almighty wanted to expose Job's weakness and foolishness and show him that He is the creator. Overwhelmed by the encounter, Job acknowledges God's limitless power and admits his own limitations and realizes God's ways are the best. God is pleased with Job's response but is upset with his friends and demands his friends take seven bulls and seven rams and go to Job and sacrifice a burnt offering for themselves. Job prays for his friends and God forgives them (see Job 42:7-9). God restores everything he had lost—health, property, and his family was built up again.

We can all see ourselves in the life of Job. We all suffer loss. We question God as to why certain things happen. We find no meaning in our suffering. When our spouse abandons us, we're left feeling empty, broken, and wanting answers. We suffer in agony as did Job. As for myself, I kept asking God "Why?" What did I do to deserve this? What could have I done differently? Wasn't I pretty enough? Didn't I do enough to make him happy? It came down to "What did I do wrong to cause the marriage to collapse?"

One piece of advice I will give you is stop asking "Why?" You will hinder your healing and drive yourself nuts in the process. You might have to face the fact that you probably will never get all your questions answered. I realize we are sometimes better off not knowing. *Let go of your need to know*. Focus on the message being offered to you through your healing process and what you cannot change. James 4:8 (NKJV) says, "Draw near to God and He will draw near to you." Humble yourselves before the Lord, and he will lift you up.

Till this very day, I do not know why my marriage ended or why I went through a three-year rebound relationship (which was as bad as my marriage) and three and a half years of unemployment. I didn't want to wallow in self-pity. I was stronger than my circumstances. I decided to pick myself up and make a commitment to move forward and not become a victim of my past but a victor because of the future God had for me. Even though I was determined not to give up, I still had to travel the rocky road of healing. I am living proof—along with thousands of other individuals—that you can recover from divorce or other life-altering events. With the help of Jesus, you must make up your mind to begin the journey of restoration.

I also wanted to prove to my ex-husband that he did not break me and my life didn't end when he left.

Admit you need help. What you don't confront, you cannot conquer. If you don't defeat your enemies, they will taunt you the rest of your life. In Jeremiah 30:17 it says, "For I will restore health to you, and your wounds I will heal, declares the Lord, because they have called you an outcast." Although the wound that divorce inflicts upon us seems incurable, know for certain God will heal you. You just have to make the decision to allow Him to.

There is one more thing you'll do well to remember (as Joyce Meyer always says), "There are no such things as drive-thru breakthroughs." When and how God choses to answer your prayers all depends on His plans for your life and how you handle and react to your situation. I can testify that you'll experience times when you will have an overwhelming desire (like a wave coming to shore) to give up and raise the white flag. But if you ask Jesus, He will give you the strength to keep on going. There will be moments when you will just want to cry. I say, cry—let it all out! Jesus understands. Even Jesus wept (see John 11:35). He knows what we have been through and the frame of mind we are in moment by moment. He is your shoulder to lean on. Be glad we don't know what tomorrow brings because we would never get out of bed or even leave our house.

People think they have absolute control over their future, but they really don't. If God would have told me that I would be going through what I did, I would have said, "No, thank you. You can skip this chapter and make it a mystery." Unfortunately, we don't have a say or a vote. God has wisely kept us in the dark about the events to come so He may instruct us to continually depend upon Him. Keep reminding yourself that this, too, shall pass.

We can learn a lot from Job. You must realize even though you may be a follower of Jesus, you will continue to experience trials. It's not like a "get out of jail free card." Jesus gave us comforting words in John 16:33 (NKJV*),* "These things I have spoken to you, that in Me you may have peace. In the world you will have tribulation; but be of good cheer, I have overcome the world." He wanted us to know that we will never be alone and He will never abandon us. He will strengthen you and give you His peace. Even though Job complained and wondered why God brought all those disasters upon him, he knew God was in control. Understand that the devil is busy working his evil on the earth. Job was confident that God would redeem him. "For I know that my Redeemer lives, and He shall stand at last on the earth" (Job 19:25 NKJV).

Job was unaware of the conversation between God and Satan. There is an invisible war raging between good and evil. Satan often inflicts suffering on humans in that battle, ever seeking to destroy them, their faith, or both. In certain cases, we will never understand why certain things happen, but all we have to remember is *God is really in control!*

All He wants from us is faith. Our responsibility to the Almighty is to obey Him, trust Him, and submit to His will. Don't ever doubt God and His grace. Just like Job claimed in 42:5 (NLT), "I had only heard about you before, but now I have seen you with my own eyes." We can know about God through what we have heard and read, but we'll only truly experience His grace when the Sovereign One reveals Himself to us at the end of the tunnel we have been traveling through. I can truly testify that I have seen God with my own eyes through the miracles He has done in and through my life. I wouldn't be where I am today if it wasn't for His love and mercy. All you have to do is surrender to His will.

Chapter 6

Live Beyond Rejection

Chapter 6

Live Beyond Rejection

Don't let anyone tell you divorce is not painful. It is devastating and it disrupts your life. Someone you loved chose to leave you. The pain can be so deep it feels as though you were sucked up by a black hole, never to return again. Becoming overwhelmed by emotions, you are like water at its boiling point, ready to explode and releasing the pressure of emotions building up inside of you. Your insides are wrenched with the feelings of betrayal and rejection. You start feeling afraid and begin thinking you will never recover.

From my own experience, I can assure you that you can overcome and be whole again. I am here to let you know, *you will pull through.* Just keep in mind, there is no set time for you to be completely restored. Don't let anyone tell you differently. There is no right or wrong way to mourn the loss of a marital bond. Everyone's recovery time is different. It's not a race. The Lord is ready to hear and listen to His children and they are never out of His sight. He will protect and keep you: "The eyes of the Lord are on the righteous, and His ears are open to their cry" (Psalms 34:15 NKJV).

I discovered that you have to grieve divorce like the death of a family member or friend. If you think about it, it's the death of an emotional, physical, and spiritual connection—something that was alive and that you nurtured. *Grief,* according to the dictionary, is "Pain of mind on account of something in the past; mental suffering arising from any cause of regret; sorrow; sadness."[3] Grief is a natural, human response to loss. Why do we grieve? Our heart is in search of a way to heal itself. Your family is broken and you don't know how to fix it. You will experience various emotions during this season in your life. Do not ignore them because doing so will cause other emotional and physical problems. I don't want to discourage you when I say this, but grief is a lonely and difficult road. This journey is not easy, and how long one grieves depends upon an individual's personality, how bad the separation or divorce was, the type of support system that is in place, and the way you found out you were no longer wanted or needed. Grief is normal, healthy, and necessary. To get through this heartache you need to feel and acknowledge this voyage of rebirth.

After accepting the truth that you have to travel a road you didn't plan for, the next step is to find a support group at church, a good Christian counselor, or a spiritually mature friend or family member. If emotions are not dealt with, they will carry over to the next relationship or resurface somewhere else. When my ex-husband left me, I was all by myself in the country with my dog. I didn't belong to a church, and the only support system I had was my parents, a really close friend, the Healing Rooms, and my Hercules. When I was home, it was just God and me. I got in the Word, prayed, fasted, and watched a variety of Christian television programs on a few Christian channels. The funny thing was I had my satellite turned off because I couldn't afford it; however, I continued receiving those particular channels. God is totally amazing! He met me right where I was and began mending my shattered life. David declared in Psalms 34:18, "The Lord is near to the brokenhearted and saves the crushed in spirit." Never forget, Jesus is our source of strength, courage, and power. He is for us, not against us (see Romans 8:31).

In both death and divorce, the bottom falls out of your world and you feel forsaken. I had never felt so rejected. It seemed as though I was a toy or some type of technology that was outdated and dismissed

3. *Websters Collegiate Dictionary*, 1913 Edition, s.v., "grief."

as inadequate or irrelevant. I could not understand how someone I loved with all my heart could turn off his love for me like a light switch. My mind automatically went to asking myself, "What did I do wrong?" or "What was not right with me?" I was ripping myself apart. Focusing on negative thoughts only made me feel worse. I was making myself believe I was a failure. That was one of the tools the devil tried using to keep me in bondage, attacking my self-worth.

The aftereffect of rejection is a very deep emotional wound. In a sense, it assigns blame, reasoning that the person who exited the relationship did so because of something you did or didn't do. It helps your spouse justify their desertion. It is the worst feeling in the world when you feel like nobody loves you or wants you. If not addressed and given the proper time to heal, it can lead to the fear of rejection by people and self-rejection. Self-rejection destroys trust and can render you emotionally incapable of getting close to other people. You begin to feel weighed down and burdened. It can further progress into loneliness, self-pity, depression, anger, hopelessness, abandonment, and guilt.

In the early stages, waves of despair come crashing down upon you. It feels like you are drowning and the life is being choked right out of you. You try to catch your breath, but you can't. You're sinking further down to the depths of the ocean floor. You are unable to cope with everyday life. It's as though the world is spinning like a kid's merry-go-round, but you are stuck and powerless to move.

There is only one healthy way of dealing with rejection so you will not live in this kind of spirit. That one thing that will help you is a relationship with Jesus. You need to fully rely on Christ. My healing process started when I accepted Jesus into my heart. I prayed, read the Word, talked to Him about how I felt, and expressed my deepest anguish. Sometimes I would just cry in His presence. He became my best friend. Don't think you always have to have it together. The writer of Psalms 88:1-3 didn't, and he expressed his feelings of hopelessness: "O Lord, God of my salvation, I cry out day and night before you. Let my prayer come before you; incline your ear to my cry! For my soul is full of troubles, and my life draws near to Sheol." You may feel like you have hit rock bottom, but you will not stay there. Bring everything to God, and He will lift you up. Remember, God is bigger than your problems. Jesus knows what you are going through. He knows what it is like to be rejected. "He came to his own, and his own people did not receive him" (John 1:11). "He was despised and rejected by men, a man of sorrows, and acquainted with grief; and as one from whom men hide their faces he was despised, and we esteemed him not" (Isaiah 53:3).

He is ready to heal you. Accept His invitation!

I have never told anyone this, but I even felt rejected during my marriage just by the words my former husband would express and the tone. There are two incidents that were burned into my memory that made me consider myself as a castaway. One is when I was unemployed for a few months. We had gone out to dinner with my parents, and right in front of them he verbally declared if I didn't get a job soon, he was no longer going to support me (this is the edited version). It was like a punch right to the stomach. I couldn't figure out why he would make such a statement—especially in the presence of my parents. I didn't respond back because I was utterly speechless. I just stared out the car window. My parents were taken aback and not too happy. They didn't know what to say either.

The second incident was when he bought his first motorcycle. We discussed before getting the bike that he needed to quit smoking so were able to make the monthly payments, and he did. But a few months later he started smoking again. After I had found out, I questioned him concerning his promise to stop smoking. His response was, "You promised me kids." That was a knockout punch to my sense of worth. It made me feel incompetent.

I didn't know how to deal with being forsaken. These little rejections culminated into the one big rejection. I really should have read the signs more instead of being in denial. It's not like it happened right out of the blue because so many things led up to the big fallout. I thought because he had no one else in his life that he would never leave me. How dumb was I for making myself believe such an illusion? I tried everything to make him happy. The worst part was doing whatever he wanted and buying whatever he wanted just to please him so he would love me in return. The plan failed; he still discarded me like trash. I started basing our relationship on performance. I found out you are only setting yourself up for a very big disappointment. No matter what I did, my ex-husband wasn't content. It really hurts when you've tried everything you could to make your spouse happy and they still leave you.

What you have to understand is that it is not about you. They are unhappy with themselves. Hurting people hurt people. I realized he was going to leave no matter what performance I put on in the stage of life. God's love for us is not performance-based but is based on who God is and that He is love. He loves you no matter what you do or how you do it. "I have loved you, my people, with an everlasting love. With unfailing love I have drawn you to myself" (Jeremiah 31:3 NLT).

As you begin the healing process, you will go through the motions of everyday life feeling numb. As I said before, acknowledge where you are at and don't live in defeat. You need to guard your heart and mind. The devil loves self-pity. Don't allow yourself to get to a point where you start thinking you can't live without your spouse or you will die. Your life is not a Romeo and Juliet play. The enemy's goal is to fill us with emotional baggage.

The most significant factor in overcoming rejection is how you react to it. It attacks our purpose and our identity. A wrong reaction to rejection can reveal that we're overly dependent on how people feel about us. This, in turn, affects our interaction with others. The truth is we were created to be loved and accepted, and the problems start when we turn exclusively and primarily to other people for that love and acceptance. God is the only ultimate and reliable source from whom we can draw our sense of identity. "But you are a chosen race, a royal priesthood, a holy nation, a people for his own possession, that you may proclaim the excellencies of him who called you out of darkness into his marvelous light" (1 Peter 2:9).

The Broken Road

My marriage was predictably unhealthy. I had to finally accept it for what it really was. It affected my life in so many aspects. After he left, part of my day would consist of thinking of ways to put my marriage back together. I would picture him doing things with his mistress that he used to do with me. I would fill myself with hatred for her. I tried making him see that I was right. But I only drove him further away. My actions only intensified my feelings of rejection. I had to stop wanting answers to my questions and stop trying to fix it on my own. You must come to terms that you will probably never get your questions answered. Eight years later, I still don't have any answers, and truthfully I don't care if I never get them because I am happy not knowing.

The aftermath of divorce is devastating and painful and the experience is cruel and degrading. It can suck the life right out of you. It's a spirit that must be dealt with before it manifests into emotional instability. Don't let the devil get a stronghold and throw you way off the road of recovery. Let God take charge of your life. If you fail to give Him control, you will live in a state of devastation the rest of your life.

I was brought to my knees. I cried out to Him to save my *marriage*, but instead God saved *me* by calling me into a relationship with His Son Jesus. Our heavenly Father revealed Himself to me, took my hand, and started leading me. Allow God to lead you on the path to freedom.

I would like you to mediate on Psalm 55. It discusses the deep dismay over the betrayal of a close friend. Sometimes the burden is too difficult to carry by yourself. What King David expresses in this psalm is how we feel sometimes after being rejected. Be like him and cry out to God and pray without ceasing.

Psalm 55 (AMP)

1 Listen to my prayer, O God, and hide not Yourself from my supplication!

2 Attend to me and answer me; I am restless *and* distraught in my complaint and must moan.

3 [And I am distracted] at the noise of the enemy, because of the oppression *and* threats of the wicked; for they would cast trouble upon me, and in wrath they persecute me.

4 My heart is grievously pained within me, and the terrors of death have fallen upon me.

5 Fear and trembling have come upon me; horror *and* fright have overwhelmed me.

6 And I say, Oh, that I had wings like a dove! I would fly away and be at rest.

7 Yes, I would wander far away, I would lodge in the wilderness. Selah [pause, and calmly think of that]!

8 I would hasten to escape *and* to find a shelter from the stormy wind and tempest.

9 Destroy [their schemes], O Lord, confuse their tongues, for I have seen violence and strife in the city.

10 Day and night they go about on its walls; iniquity and mischief are in its midst.

11 Violence *and* ruin are within it; fraud and guile do not depart from its streets *and* marketplaces.

12 For it is not an enemy who reproaches *and* taunts me—then I might bear it; nor is it one who has hated me who insolently vaunts himself against me—then I might hide from him.

13 But it was you, a man my equal, my companion and my familiar friend.

14 We had sweet fellowship together and used to walk to the house of God in company.

15 Let desolations *and* death come suddenly upon them; let them go down alive to Sheol (the place of the dead), for evils are in their habitations, in their hearts, *and* their inmost part.

16 As for me, I will call upon God, and the Lord will save me.

[17] Evening and morning and at noon will I utter my complaint and moan *and* sigh, and He will hear my voice.

[18] He has redeemed my life in peace from the battle that was against me [so that none came near me], for they were many who strove with me.

[19] God will hear and humble them, even He Who abides of old—Selah [pause, and calmly think of that]!—because in them there has been no change [of heart], and they do not fear, revere, *and* worship God.

[20] [My companion] has put forth his hands against those who were at peace with him; he has broken *and* profaned his agreement [of friendship and loyalty].

[21] The words of his mouth were smoother than cream *or* butter, but war was in his heart; his words were softer than oil, yet they were drawn swords.

[22] Cast your burden on the Lord [releasing the weight of it] and He will sustain you; He will never allow the [consistently] righteous to be moved (made to slip, fall, or fail).

[23] But You, O God, will bring down the wicked into the pit of destruction; men of blood and treachery shall not live out half their days. But I will trust in, lean on, *and* confidently rely on You.

My final point is this: In order to gain influence, the spirit of rejection distorts everything that occurs in our lives into feelings of acceptance or rejection. It keeps the focus on ourselves instead of turning to God for the love we need, which only He can provide. Remember, don't allow rejection to define who you are or your actions. Rejection is about you not measuring up to someone's subjective attitude or actions. Who says he or she is right? Other people do not determine your worth—God does!

Chapter 7

God: Our Therapy for Anger

Chapter 7

God: Our Therapy for Anger

Anger. What springs to mind when you hear the word? Probably several things because there are so many sources that convey this uncomfortable response to our environment, and it has a wide range of intensity too. We all experience it. Anger in and of itself is not sin; it serves a useful purpose. God gave us our emotions. However, what caused our anger and how we handle this wild beast determines if it is sin or not. The most important thing is to deal with our anger in a righteous and godly manner.

Anger is often an emotional response related to one's psychological interpretation of having been threatened. A lot of our fury develops from our circumstances. Reaction to anger is dependent upon a person's individual characteristics and their pre-anger state. This corrosive emotion can be displayed either passively or aggressively.

God is angry at sin because it separates us from Him. Jesus was angry at the Pharisees because of their hardened hearts. He also became angry when He found men selling goods in the temple courts. Yet, when Jesus was angry He never sinned. That is called righteous anger. We also can handle this emotion without sinning too. "Be angry and do not sin; do not let the sun go down on your anger, and give no opportunity to the devil" (Ephesians 4:26-27). When we give Satan that opportunity, it blocks out the light and strips us of any confidence in overcoming a certain problem.

The rage you are likely experiencing is an expression of grief after a loss. After some devastating event, you start asking the questions like, "Why is this happening to me?" or, "Who is to blame?" For our own self-satisfaction, we have to find the purpose or reason why our spouse left us. We look for something or someone to blame. It is important for people to feel acknowledged when they are hurting. When I had to interact with my ex-husband I tried to bring my wrath down upon him. I wanted to let him know that he severely wounded me. On the contrary, it didn't serve a purpose. It only caused him to be angrier and he could have cared less about my pain. I wanted to be compensated for the wrong that was committed against me. When we become the judge we are putting ourselves before God. We don't think God can handle our problems. We want justice now. Remember, "'Vengeance is Mine, I will repay,' says the Lord" (Romans 12:19 NKJV). Our heavenly Father will correct the wrongs that have been done to us, but it will be done His way and in His timing.

When someone gets mad, they can lose their temper and display it outwardly. When rage begins consuming them and goes beyond their ability of self-control, they explode and therefore give themselves permission to rant. It's more important for them to win and assert their position. If not kept in check, it can build up to a possible physical attack against the person with whom they are upset or anyone or anything around them at that moment. It is best to manage your anger and not let it linger for a long period of time because it could go to a level you will regret.

Take note of what James (Jesus' brother) says in James 1:19-20 (NLT), "Understand this, my dear brothers and sisters: You must all be quick to listen, slow to speak, and slow to get angry. Human anger does not produce the righteousness God desires." Not only was I enraged at my ex-husband, but I was filled with hatred toward "the other woman." I had a lot of violent thoughts toward her, and I felt happy about it. I had dreams of physical harm coming to her. I wanted her to pay for what she did. I would verbally attack her when discussing my situation with my family and friends. Down the road I learned that these actions were hurting me—not her. She could have cared less about me and how I felt (even though she went through the same thing prior to snatching him away from me). She got what she wanted—my husband.

On the other hand, some people hold their anger inside. Keeping anger bottled up is called anger repression. Some people feel they shouldn't say anything because they believe it is better than blowing up. However, allowing anger to fester inside won't help either. This can lead to a deep stronghold of bitterness, resentment, and hatred. Furthermore, not expressing your anger in a godly way can develop into physical health issues. Some of these issues include headaches, depression, insomnia, digestion problems, increased anxiety, and heart attacks to name a few. Putting a lid on your anger can lead to an eruption of unresolved struggles. When a volcano is ready to erupt, the earth's plates collide causing the rock underneath to melt. As magma pushes upward, it melts more rock. The hot magma collects underneath the earth's surface. As the magma increases, the pressure can become so great that the only place for the magma to go is outward. Just like the volcanic eruption, if we keep our anger inside, all the bitterness, resentment, and malice will get to a point where we can no longer keep it inside. This is when we have reached our pressure point and the only release is out. You need to look to God for help. If you don't start dealing with it, it can become difficult to overcome. Ecclesiastes 7:9 says, "Be not quick in your spirit to become angry, for anger lodges in the heart of fools."

My anger not only turned to violent thoughts toward her, but I lashed out verbally at my ex. I would bring everything up that he had done to me, even things that had occurred at the beginning of our relationship. I couldn't hurt him physically, but I could emotionally. I called him names and said things just to aggravate him. I thought it was a form of retaliation. But my immature behavior only made matters worse—it caused the war to escalate. He became infuriated and the conflicts became more intense. At the time, I thought I was making him see "the errors of his ways." Of course, it didn't work; he still thought he had done nothing wrong. I don't know how he justified his blindness to the truth; only God knows. He didn't feel bad or show any remorse. Consequently, I became more incensed.

I truly wanted revenge. Retribution is the world's way, but it is not God's way. "Do not say, 'I will do to him as he has done to me; I will pay the man back for what he has done'" (Proverbs 24:29). Instead, remember what our heavenly Father told the Israelites in Leviticus 19:18, "You shall not take vengeance or bear a grudge against the sons of your own people, but you shall love your neighbor as yourself: I am the Lord."

There are healthy ways to control your anger. The best way, of course, is God's way. I have heard it said we should vent our anger and get it out of our system; we will feel better. It is supposed to release tension. It is like you are trying to get people to listen to you. You think, "If I don't get angry, I am letting my ex get away with what he did to me." But by doing this you are tearing apart your family even further. Yelling and screaming at each other and becoming verbally abusive can be detrimental and is definitely not beneficial. Whatever is said or done can never be taken back. The Bible says, "Fools vent their anger, but the wise quietly hold it back" (Proverbs 29:11 NLT). In other words, a wise man will not utter everything in his mind. He will refrain for a more suitable time. Our words and deeds are controlled by our thoughts. It says in Matthew 15:18 (NLT), "But the words you speak come from the heart—that's what defiles you."

Do not mistakenly believe that anger cannot be controlled. God doesn't command the impossible. If we really want to, we can keep it under control. Imagine yourself being in a fit of rage when your pastor rings your doorbell. Your demeanor would change real quickly! Anger *is* controllable. We have the ability to be in command of our anger just like Jesus was. Jesus became angry at times and was tempted in every way like we are, but He did not sin (Hebrews 4:15). What we need to do is look for the way of escape. You need to repent and ask God for forgiveness and pray to overcome the temptation to lose your temper. According to 1 Corinthians 10:13, "No temptation has overtaken you that is not common to man. God is faithful, and he will not let you be tempted beyond your ability, but with the temptation he will also provide the way of escape, that you may be able to endure it." In other words, God is our escape hatch. To overcome anger, you need to admit you are angry and you need to make up your mind that you will change. If you decide to have a dialogue with your former spouse, pray to God beforehand. Your spouse might want to say things to get you upset. It is always good to be prepared.

Over time and with God's help, I made the decision not to let what my ex-husband said to me affect my response. The devil wants you living in constant turmoil. Don't let him win.

Another beneficial step is get into God's Word. Psalms 119:105 is true: "Your word is a lamp to my feet and a light to my path." The revelation of God's Word provides the insight to guide us. We will not stumble in the darkness if we mediate on His Word. When Jesus was in the desert for forty days and forty nights Satan tried to tempt Him. Jesus handled Satan's attacks by quoting Scripture. Make a list of verses related to anger or whatever the situation may be that you are going through at that moment. Memorize the verses and declare them in Jesus' name. When you start feeling "hot under the collar," quote Scripture by speaking it aloud. I guarantee you will start feeling peace.

Because you have legal matters to deal with, you should develop an action plan to prevent any detrimental outbursts. As I previously stated before, read the Word and pray in private or with a friend. The wise and righteous recognize the need to weigh matters carefully before acting or reacting (see Proverbs 15:28). My ex-husband could be volatile at times and become confrontational. Before I became a follower of Jesus Christ and started changing my thoughts, I would feed into his attitude and become confrontational as well. I always wanted to get the last word in just to prove I was right or just get one over on him. Remember, "A soft answer turns away wrath, but a harsh word stirs up anger" (Proverbs 15:1). It doesn't say we should clam up and give no answer. When you give an answer, be calm. I noticed that when I responded peacefully to my ex, it would defuse the situation. You are capable of speaking in a tone that expresses your displeasure, but not in a way that is hurtful or antagonistic. However, there would be times I was calm and he still would raise his voice. Just to prove I was in control of my reactions, I would just let him say whatever he wanted without doing the same. I wanted to break the cycle of "tit for tat."

It is inevitable that you will have to interact with your soon-to-be ex-spouse, so only speak what is necessary. Don't say whatever comes to mind—speak to help, not to hurt. Meditate on Ephesians 4:29, "Let no corrupting talk come out of your mouths, but only such as is good for building up, as fits the occasion, that it may give grace to those who hear." One way you can put off the old and put on the new is by dealing with uncontrolled anger and becoming self-controlled. Be willing to listen. It will make things go smoother and can prove to be really beneficial.

After the spirit of rejection punches you in the gut, anger is part of the healing process. However, don't let it get the best of you. Don't allow it to consume you and bury you in darkness. Don't let your pride minimize your anger's wrong. Doing so makes exceptions and excuses for your anger. Get help. Release your anger to God. It's a moment-by-moment reliance on Him. "That according to the riches of his glory he may grant you to be strengthened with power through his Spirit in your inner being" (Ephesians 3:16). Remember, the Spirit of God empowers you to do the impossible. You need to let go and let God. I call that faith.

Chapter 8

Dealing with Depression, Hope in God

Chapter 8

Dealing with Depression, Hope in God

Dealing with the dangers of life,

Each day alone through stress and strife,

Praying to God to sort it out,

Remembering what brought it about.

Every day in lives tough test,

Securing a future nevertheless.

Seeing its secrets and letting them go,

In a life itself and the world we know.

Only thinking that maybe someday,

Nice things will happen like peace we pray.

"Come to me, all who labor and are heavy laden, and I will give you rest" (Matthew 11:28).

The rest Jesus promises is love, healing, and peace with the Holy Father. God's peace is different from the world's peace. True peace is not found in positive thinking, in the absence of conflict, in good feelings, or in everything going our way. True peace is found in

Christ. Jesus declares, "I have said these things to you, that in me you may have peace" (John 16:33). It is an awareness of sufficiency and serenity regardless of life's circumstances. It is experiencing joy in the midst of unhappiness. What we put in our minds determines what comes out in our words and actions. Peace has a lot to do with your focus. It states in Proverbs 23:7 (AMPC), "For as he thinks in his heart, so is he." If you continually meditate and focus on the loss of your marriage, you will become depressed and feel abandoned. Keep in mind that loneliness is depression's faithful partner. By focusing on your mental state, you have defined yourself by your mindset of unworthiness.

Depression is a natural response to loss and rejection. It is characterized by feelings of severe despondency and dejection. It is typically followed by feelings of inadequacy and guilt. It's an upheaval of a person's normal existence. But it will not last forever. It might be hard to believe, but it is part of the healing process. However, if we give it permission to take root, we start a negative thinking pattern where you can't imagine anything good happening. As a result, we begin to lose focus of our daily lives. When we cooperate with these fickle emotions, the depression and the loneliness goes deeper and we begin to shut down. Sometimes we get to the point where we become numb and don't feel anything.

Looking back at my situation, I even got to the point where I didn't want to eat or be in the presence of other people. All I wanted to do was lie in bed and wallow in the mud of my own self-pity. I realized that God did not want me loathing my existence. I took the first step (as slow as it was) and moved forward with my life. I was not going to let divorce define me. Understand that people are going to hurt each other and let each other down. Don't allow this dark veil of gloom cover you.

When you start feeling depressed about your divorce, you begin feeling sad. You are yearning for the marriage you lost and the dreams imagined unfulfilled. You begin to feel as though no one will want you. You feel unworthy of love and think you will be alone forever. In a sense, you believe you are damaged goods. I certainly did. I thought I was incapable of handling mature relationships. I started believing the devil's lies. We feel like Jeremiah did when he had to relay God's message of destruction to the people for their sins: "Woe is me because of my hurt! My wound is grievous. But I said, 'Truly this is an affliction, and I must bear it'" (Jeremiah 10:19). Just as Jeremiah is lamenting for his people, we are lamenting over our grief. In order to "bear it," we must have the patience to let God do what pleases Him (see 1 Samuel 3:18). Don't let your circumstance change your view of God. He knows how to direct our paths better than we do.

The void left by your spouse is real—a painful reminder of the complexity of the marriage bond. It may feel unbearable at times, but let it be something that draws you closer to Jesus. Bear in mind, the devil uses fear to keep us feeling depressed and lonely. He wants to keep you in a lifetime of guilt, condemnation, and self-hatred. You need to reach out to God to be whole again.

When I was depressed, our gracious Father showed me that He was all I needed, and this is still true today. I know we all want someone tangible to love, but you must realize that God doesn't always permit this to happen when we want it. I recognize we live in a couples-oriented society, but be aware of the fact that God is using this time to get you closer to Him. It is in the dark moments when you are forced to make faith-led decisions. We are spiritual beings, and we need more of Jesus. Consider being by yourself in this season of your life as a gift to get to know our Lord and Savior better. I suggest reflecting on Psalms 46:1, "God is our refuge and strength, a very present help in trouble."

By focusing on your relationship with God, it will allow you to reflect on the failure of your marriage. It will give you insight to what worked and what didn't work. I heard somewhere that when you are depressed and lonely you don't have the mental focus to realize you're exaggerating your shortcomings. Consider what the apostle Paul said in Philippians 3:13, "Brothers, I do not consider that I have made it my own. But one thing I do: forgetting what lies behind and straining forward to what lies ahead." You need to stop feeling sorry for yourself and begin praising Christ for being with you and meeting your needs. Our hope is in Jesus, so we can let go of past guilt and look forward to what God will help us become. Don't linger in the past. While you are experiencing the grieving process, you will need to rediscover yourself. Two things you must not do are to worship your feelings and isolate yourself. All it does is reinforce the depression. A Christian's life should be based on the truth of God's Word, not feelings. "Draw near to God, and he will draw near to you" (James 4:8). Humble yourself before the Lord, and tell Him everything you are feeling.

Another good plan is develop same-sex friendships and seek godly counsel. It will develop emotional stability. There are more strategies you can take to overcome depression and loneliness. There was a study published in the *Journal of Health and Social Behavior* pointing to the fact that twenty percent of divorced and widowed people are more likely to develop chronic health issues. First and foremost, you need to take care of yourself. You need to eat healthy meals, get enough sleep, and get adequate exercise. Believe it or not, it will help ease your emotional stress.

An additional step is developing a "get moving" strategy. This might be out of the box, but consider changing your routine. Plan something you have been aspiring to do. Get involved in church and help other people in need. It will help you as well because you won't be focused on yourself and your circumstance and God will heal you in the process. Keep in mind, when we receive comfort we can pass it on. Furthermore, you must catch negative thoughts, think positively, eliminate lies—and the most freeing mental exercise is forgiveness. I know what you are thinking: *I don't think so*. I realize you might be at a point where you are not ready yet, and that is perfectly fine. Just keep seeking God and ask Him to help you in this area. I will touch on this subject a little later.

Do not dread the journey or deny the pain you are experiencing. If you reject the pain you will only have to deal with it later. You will be like a leaky hose. The repressed feelings will start leaking into other areas of your life. Don't forget God is here to help you. Don't stay stuck in the past. You need to be better, not bitter. Don't let depression and loneliness blind you and distort the authenticity of life. Don't waste your life living for people's acceptance; you will die from their rejection.

Candy Block

Decide to be a victor and not a victim. Bitterness corrodes and eats away at you little by little. It is a state of mind that willfully holds on to angry feelings, ready to take offense and ready to break out in anger at any moment. It can lead to intense hatred and hinders the willingness to forgive. It also prevents possible reconciliation. We need to be vigilant about allowing God to heal us. You don't want to live in bondage all your life. Ask God to help change your attitude.

I never had children, but I look at the pain of divorce as a woman going through childbirth. When labor pains begin, they become very intense and unbearable for a period of time. Sometimes you feel like giving up and you just can't take it anymore. Then the baby finally arrives. After the baby is born and you are holding him or her in your arms, you realize all that pain was worth it. God wants us to realize the intense heartache will be worth it because what He has waiting for us in the end is beautiful and well worth the wait. David cried out in Psalm 143 (NLT):

1 Hear my prayer, O LORD;
listen to my plea!
Answer me because you are faithful and righteous.
2 Don't put your servant on trial,
for no one is innocent before you.
3 My enemy has chased me.
He has knocked me to the ground
and forces me to live in darkness like those in the grave.
4 I am losing all hope;
I am paralyzed with fear.
5 I remember the days of old.
I ponder all your great works
and think about what you have done.
6 I lift my hands to you in prayer.
I thirst for you as parched land thirsts for rain.
7 Come quickly, LORD, and answer me,
for my depression deepens.

Don't turn away from me,
or I will die.
8 Let me hear of your unfailing love each morning,
for I am trusting you.
Show me where to walk,
for I give myself to you.
9 Rescue me from my enemies, LORD;
I run to you to hide me.
10 Teach me to do your will,
for you are my God.
May your gracious Spirit lead me forward
on a firm footing.
11 For the glory of your name, O LORD, preserve my life.
Because of your faithfulness, bring me out of this distress.
12 In your unfailing love, silence all my enemies
and destroy all my foes,
for I am your servant.

David was distraught because he was in danger. He had people pursuing him and wanting to take his life. Just like the great psalmist, our spirits become weak; we lose hope and we're caught in paralyzing fear and stuck in deep depression. We feel like we are unable to pull ourselves out of this vortex of emotions. But with God's help, we can do it. David cried out to God. Do what he did by reaching out to our Redeemer in prayer, trusting Him and being committed to doing His will.

Chapter 9

A New Relationship, Not a Cure for Loneliness

Chapter 9

A New Relationship, Not a Cure for Loneliness

"The most terrible poverty is loneliness and the feeling of being unloved." —Mother Teresa

The death of a marriage creates many gaps in our preplanned, routine, and predictable lives. It is hard to adjust to the loss of companionship, love, and security that are a key part of marriage. The Bible speaks of marriage as two becoming one flesh. The ripping apart of the marriage, therefore, makes it feel like an amputation. The sudden absence of this intimacy is very painful. One of the resulting emotions is loneliness. Consequently, we begin desiring a new relationship.

An essential foundation for personal and spiritual growth is to make sure you know the difference between knowing what you want and what you need. I will get straight to the point: do not get into a new relationship right after your divorce or separation. It will hinder and slow down your healing process. When you force-fit someone rather than wait, you create more pain, and it shows you are willing to compromise. Let God heal you. "You make known to me the path of life; in your presence there is fullness of joy; at your right hand are pleasures forevermore" (Psalms 16:11). Rest assured God is close at hand in times of need. God meets our needs by His presence and by spending time with other believers, not a new relationship.

When making a decision regarding a new relationship, do not make it based on your feelings. Your feelings are fickle and irrational at times. Your future relationship is only as good as what you bring to it. I suggest praying Psalms 139:23-24, “Search me, O God, and know my heart! Try me and know my thoughts! And see if there be any grievous way in me, and lead me in the way everlasting!” Trust God enough to invite Him to examine your feelings and motives. If you allow God this exploration, you will continue on the path He has set before you. Starting a new journey with someone new when you are not whole yet is like taking pieces from a puzzle and forcing them together. It is not going to work and the picture will never be complete. Do not take less then God’s best. You are only setting yourself up for relational failure again. Selfishness causes this desperation for a new relationship, and you will likely repeat the same mistakes.

That is exactly what happened to me. While adding salt to the already festering wound of my failed marriage, toward the end of 2007 (after filing for divorce) I got into a relationship I shouldn’t have. I met a man at the Healing Rooms while going to receive prayer every week for the restoration of my marriage. He would come almost every week with the men from a substance abuse recovery program. In the beginning he seemed very sweet and likable. At the time, I didn’t realize he had his own issues he was struggling with and had not defeated. This relationship was a no-no and doomed from the start. I wasn’t divorced yet and I wasn’t healed; I wasn’t in a state of mind to begin a new emotional connection. As a matter of fact, he wasn’t prepared either.

This friendship began as we talked with each other at The Healing Rooms, and then it grew to talking with each other on the phone about our pasts and what we wanted for the future. I was being led by my feelings. It made me overlook the fact I was going through a traumatic event. He made me feel wanted and not rejected. We were both blinded by our desires. We both heard what we wanted to.

This relationship was not God-ordained. I strongly feel this man was put in my path for a reason, but not the ones I thought. As the relationship grew we brought it to a level that God didn't plan. I didn't turn inward and consider what I could or couldn't bring to the relationship. I didn't have the emotional stability to handle a new relationship. It detoured the restoration of the person God wanted me to become. I was empty and had nothing to give. I don't believe I was even at a point to assess the areas of my life where I needed to grow. I didn't distinguish between what I wanted and what I needed.

I believe my new friend wanted to take this relationship further than I wanted to or intended to. I sense now the relationship continued because I mistook gratitude for love. He was generous enough to replace two floors in my house and fix my well pump. As time progressed, he began turning into a person other than what he portrayed. He was jealous of my ex-husband, jealous of other men, angry I wasn't over my marriage, and he began assertively pushing marriage for our near future. This occurred within six months of the relationship beginning. Then his drug addiction and his desire not to work started revealing itself. Subsequently, he started asking me to pay for his pain medications (which he really didn't need). He turned out to be like my ex-husband, and in some cases worse. When I wouldn't do or give him what he wanted, he would get mad and we would fight. He even moved a few times from one state to another and then back again. I helped him financially with the transportation to come back. How blinded was I?

As time progressed, the relationship just kept getting worse and more demanding. My involvement with him was taking it's toll on me. Not only was I trying to heal from a failed marriage, but I was dealing with this toxic relationship I should have never permitted to develop. The only reason I didn't end it sooner was because I didn't want to make him feel as rejected as I did. After three years, I was at my breaking point. I kept praying to God to end it because I wasn't physically or emotionally strong enough to do it on my own.

What broke the camel's back was when he wanted a marriage commitment. I just couldn't. My heart wasn't in it and I really didn't love him. It ended around Thanksgiving of 2010. He was still demanding a commitment from me that I did not want to give him. I told him no and that it was over.

I felt bad, not only for myself but for him too. I was trying to put a bandage over a gaping wound by getting into this relationship. I didn't want to drag it on any longer. It became too complicated for me to handle. I really didn't want to hurt him, but I had to think of myself and my future. The only way I could heal was placing it in Jesus' hands. By letting go and letting God, I could move forward and recover from both my marriage and this failed relationship. Nothing was blocking my road to healing now. All I had to do was focus on my relationship with our almighty Father. Our gracious God proved to me He was all I needed.

Our focus should be on the healing aspect of our journey. Remember, you do not have the emotional and physical energy to make wise decisions. You are hurt and you want compensation, but you must allow the wounds to fade away with the sunset never to rise again. "This is what the LORD says—your Redeemer, the Holy One of Israel: 'I am the LORD your God, who teaches you what is good for you and leads you along the paths you should follow'" (Isaiah 48:17 NLT). There is no way God can teach us what is best for us and direct our path if we are unwilling to surrender to Him completely. Allow God to lead you because, most likely, the rebound relationship will end like a train wreck. Subsequently, you will be left with more pain. You have two broken people coming together with all their baggage full of hurt with sky-high expectations of a redemptive romance. Nothing can be added if you are both broken. Then all your efforts become very draining, and you break under the pressure. You will end up worse off than before, not better.

Let Jesus be your life coach; work together with Him and you will start seeing people differently. Set your priorities and make guidelines. You don't want to be attracted to the same type of person your former spouse was. The same dysfunction can draw two people toward each other. By allowing God to heal you, you will not be drawn to that complimentary personality. Take time and work on the most important relationship, your relationship with God. Learn to improve yourself and realize that you are a whole person in Christ and not half of something. This is when you begin to see the possibility of having the kind of relationship with God you never had before. Don't pressure yourself because there is no set time to date. You are ready to date when you have something beneficial to offer, and when you don't need someone to complete you.

Another important issue is trust. As God heals you, you will learn to trust again. I realize it is easier said than done, but it is possible if you consent to God taking control and rebuilding you. That was the last big issue I had to conquer. Even with my current husband, I permitted myself to be suspicious of everything he said and everything he did—as well as everything he didn't say or do. I was making myself anxious and worried for nothing. I didn't want to be that person anymore. Then I prayed and gave it up to God, and over a period of time I finally conquered the demon of mistrust. Do not become mistrustful and fearful of being hurt again. Mistrust can come in many forms, from suspecting infidelity to fearing he or she will abandon you emotionally and physically. Don't think all members of the opposite sex are like your ex-spouse. They are not, and it is not fair to either them or yourself to go into a new relationship with preconceived notions. In addition, don't put a wall up where you don't allow anyone to enter. Don't take charge of protecting yourself; that is God's job.

The quintessential victory in overcoming loneliness is understanding the difference between the grieving process and the spirit of grief that will try to attach itself to the hurting person. The natural process of grief will help the person get better, but the spirit of grief will cause the person to get worse and go deeper into despair. But in God's infinite wisdom, He didn't plan marriage to be the only solution to loneliness. Nobody but God can fill the spiritual void within you. God has given us His people to be our family, and He provides that through His church.

God can use transitions in our lives to open doors to new experiences, but we must be willing to let go of our feelings and move on. You can learn to be content. Recall that while Jesus was on the cross he cried out,

The Broken Road

“My God, My God, why have You forsaken Me?” Jesus knows how you feel right now. He will meet you in your loneliest place and help you. Despite your feelings, God is near. God is enough! Believe new seasons of your life will come.

Pray for courage. It helps us to withstand and grow through ongoing pain, suffering, isolation, and related difficulties. “For God has not given us a spirit of fear, but of power and of love and of a sound mind” (2 Timothy 1:7 NKJV). When we allow people and situations to intimidate us, we neutralize our efforts to recover and reestablish our purpose. The power of the Holy Spirit can help us overcome our fear of what some people may say or do to us. Take control by allowing God to take control. I wrote this little prayer, which is worth reciting:

Dear Father, forgive me of the selfish desire to worship my feelings of loneliness and self-pity, thus ignoring Your plan and purpose for my life. I feel as though I am nothing. Lord; help me to let go of me and only see You. I know You are not the God of confusion. I pray for You to restore all that is broken within me. I yearn to be whole and free. Draw me close to You. Give me faith; give me trust to know that You will lead the way. Let my faith rise. I ask You to give me the heart to fight. Please tell my heart to beat again.

Chapter 10

Unforgiveness: The Spiritual Poison

Chapter 10

Unforgiveness: The Spiritual Poison

"Unforgiveness is like drinking a poison and expecting someone else to die from it." —Unknown.

Would you ever consider unforgiveness as a disease or a deadly poison? I don't think anyone really would.

Yet it is one of the more popular tools the devil uses against God's people. Not wanting to forgive is, in essence, hatred. It is torture having hateful thoughts rolling around in your head. It has far-reaching and unexpected consequences. Although unforgiveness starts in the mind, it doesn't stay quarantined to our thinking. Believe it or not, it can lead to many illnesses. Unforgiveness is a heavy burden to carry.

If you want full restoration, forgiveness is the key to healing. Do you want an effective prayer life? Do you want God to forgive you? Then break the barrier and forgive. You might not feel like it, but if you want to move forward, you have to take the leap of faith. "And whenever you stand praying, forgive, if you have anything against anyone, so that your Father also who is in heaven may forgive you your trespasses" (Mark 11:25). Don't be one of those people who would rather do something distasteful than offer forgiveness. Give it to God; transfer all the hurts and wrongdoings to our heavenly Father. It is all about you and your relationship with God. It will open the door to a new life.

I discovered the first step to forgiving is forgiving yourself. You may be asking "Why should I forgive myself?" We have a tendency to hold ourselves more accountable than we do others. It takes more energy to hold resentment toward ourselves than toward other people. You have to keep in mind that both you and your spouse played a part in the dissolution of this holy covenant. For example, in my previous marriage, my ex-husband murdered the union, but I was an accomplice. You are freeing yourself when you turn inward and forgive the role you acted out in the play called *My Life*. It will bring you peace. Once you have forgiven yourself, you can take the next step and forgive the person who hurt you.

You are probably thinking, *How can I forgive my husband or wife after what they did to me?* The ability to pardon someone is not based on a feeling; if it were, we would never do it. Forgiveness has to be a conscious decision. People think that they are letting the offender off the hook, but you are really the beneficiary. If you complicate your healing by not forgiving, then the ability to move forward will be even more difficult, if not unattainable.

One very important thing to remember is that forgiveness is not a sign of weakness. It is a sign of strength—it shows that you truly love God. By not forgiving, you are telling God you don't trust Him to take care of matters. In essence, you are taking the place of God and becoming the judge. *Judging* means "to form an opinion by comparison of facts, qualities, or ideas."[4] Therefore, by not forgiving you are condemning the person and denying forgiveness. You don't want to become the judge because you will be crushed under the burden. Keep in mind, by releasing your anger and responsibility (desire) to judge (which you placed on yourself), you recognize that God is the official magistrate. You give God back the right to take care of justice. Jesus says, "Do not judge others, and you will not be judged. For you will be treated as you treat others. The standard you use in judging is the standard by which you will be judged. And why worry about a speck in your friend's eye when you have a log in your own?" (Matthew 7:1-3 NLT).

---

4. *Websters Collegiate Dictionary*, 1913 Edition, s.v., "judge."

Candy Block

We need to judge ourselves before we judge others because we are guilty of similar or worse faults. What would happen if God judged as we think people deserved to be judged? The true and living God is the only one with the right to judge. He knows a person's heart. When you judge someone, you always put yourself in a position of being more righteous.

When you don't forgive and hold on to the bitterness and resentment, it can affect you physically. Unforgiveness is basically the inability to deliberate decision; to not forgive someone who hurt you. It is essentially a stress response with potential health consequences. It can lead to ulcers, high blood pressure, heart disease, sleeplessness, and a host of other illnesses and diseases. Science has finally caught up with what the Bible says about the unwillingness to forgive. It says in Proverbs 18:14 (NKJV), "The spirit of a man will sustain him in sickness; but who can bear a broken spirit?" Our health depends on mental and spiritual serenity. It is very advantageous to keep our minds calm. A discontented spirit makes your appearance look gloomy. You must understand unforgiveness is disobedience to God. Deuteronomy 28:15-68 describes all the curses that would come upon the Israelites if they disobeyed Him. It is the same for us today; if we do not keep God's commandments, we will forfeit all of His blessings as well. What a tragedy that would be.

Unforgiveness doesn't merely alter our physical health; it can hinder our spiritual well-being. Furthermore, it can block God from answering prayers, and blessings can be withheld from us. We become spiritually dull and are no longer an effective witness.

It keeps us jailed to the past, and our lives become consumed with unforgiveness each time we give thought to the offender who caused our misery. As a result, we feed the spiritual stronghold trying to impede our future. Don't act foolishly and think that by not forgiving your former spouse, you are punishing them. The truth is you are not. You are punishing yourself by putting yourself in prison and giving them the key. All our attempts to reach great things will ultimately end in failure, heartbreak, and ruin. John 15:5 tells us if we abide in Christ we will produce much spiritual fruit. If we don't abide in Christ by keeping His commandments, how do you expect Him to hear your prayers? True wisdom is measured by a person's character. How are you acting?

It took me several times to forgive my ex-husband, and even longer to forgive the "other woman." Yes, believe it or not, I finally forgave her. It took me two years. I blamed her for everything that happened. As time went on, I realized he was just as much a part of it as she was. I learned if I was going to have any kind of peaceful existence, it was essential to forgive her as well as him. Remember, forgiveness is a process, not an event.

I understood my ex-husband wasn't the true enemy. The real perpetrator was Satan. "For we are not fighting against flesh-and-blood enemies, but against evil rulers and authorities of the unseen world, against mighty powers in this dark world, and against evil spirits in the heavenly places" (Ephesians 6:12 NLT). These mighty powers are demons, and Satan has control over them. They are very real and powerful. Their main goal is to make us as ineffective for Christ as possible. They will use any and every device possible to turn us from God back to sin. The evil one has numerous ways of deceiving unstable souls. His demons strike before we are aware of them. We need to be strong through God's Holy Spirit because we have to engage in these struggles until Christ returns, though in the end we are assured victory.

Please do not confuse trust with forgiveness. Forgiveness is not the same as trust. After such a life-altering event as divorce it is hard to trust the person who betrayed you or, for that matter, anyone else. You will never forget what has been done to you, but forgiving is releasing them from the prison you placed them in (your mind) and canceling the debt. By doing so, you are allowing Jesus to take control and handle the situation according to His will and purpose. Trust can be restored with God's help, especially if reconciliation is involved.

Unfortunately, there are times when it is broken beyond repair, and in certain circumstances it is not even wise to pursue reconciliation. We can pray for the person from a distance without putting ourselves in hurtful situations. Jesus was the most forgiving, loving man who ever lived, but He knew He could not trust all people. He knew their hearts (see John 2:24). Some people will never change, so we need to change how we respond and quit expecting them to be any different.

Jesus needs to be our standard. There is right and there is sin. Sin is wrong even if we think it is right. We must remember that all of God's people have been unfaithful to Him—from the Israelites down to us in this present world.

Do you want the Creator of the universe to forgive you? We have sinned worse toward God than people have sinned against us. When Jesus is not our model, we are looser with our tongues and we become less mindful of our actions.

> Since God chose you to be the holy people he loves, you must clothe yourselves with tenderhearted mercy, kindness, humility, gentleness, and patience. Make allowance for each other's faults, and forgive anyone who offends you. Remember, the Lord forgave you, so you must forgive others. Above all, clothe yourselves with love, which binds us all together in perfect harmony. And let the peace that comes from Christ rule in your hearts. For as members of one body you are called to live in peace. And always be thankful
>
> (Colossians 3:12-15 NLT).

Forgiveness breaks down walls, has no limitations, and is not selective. In Matthew 18, Peter asked Jesus how many times we should forgive others. Jesus replied, "I do not say to you seven times, but seventy-seven times" (Matthew 18:22). The point Jesus was making is never stop forgiving and do not even keep a scoreboard of how many times we forgive someone. It doesn't look good. It seems as though you have set a limit, and once you reach it you will stop forgiving. We are usually careless about forgiveness until we are put into a situation where we need it ourselves. God honors our obedience to Him when we choose to forgive. He completes the work in His time. Our goal is to keep forgiving by faith until the work of forgiveness is completed in our hearts by the Holy Spirit.

The Broken Road

Practicing forgiveness allows you to receive love and mercy as well as God's forgiveness. It makes you realize our Comforter is everywhere at all times, and love is all there is. It will remove the blinders from your eyes to see the wonder of God in your life.

It takes courage and strength to exonerate the wrongdoer. It allows you to be an overcomer and not a victim. The deeper the hurt, the more time it will take to forgive. Do not get discouraged if it takes longer than you expected. Jehovah will be with you every step of this voyage of restoration. Go somewhere in private and admit to Jesus any anger, bitterness, resentment, or unforgiveness you are harboring. Lay all your burdens at the cross. "Take My yoke upon you and learn from Me, for I am gentle and lowly in heart, and *you will find rest for your souls*. For My yoke is easy and My burden is light" (Matthew 11:29-30 NKJV). The rest Jesus talks about is love, healing, and peace with God. A relationship with God transforms meaningless worry into a new purpose. Concede and tell Jesus you cannot do it on your own. He will personally start mending your shattered heart. He did mine.

Chapter 11

Moving Ahead: The New Normal

Chapter 11

Moving Ahead: The New Normal

Are you more optimistic about your future? Hopefully you are not feeling like the past is determining what is yet to come?

Once you forgive yourself and your former spouse, the healing process is still not totally complete. After the initial shock and the emotional meltdown, you need to stop having a pity party and allow the caterpillar in you to turn into a beautiful butterfly. "We do this by keeping our eyes on Jesus, the champion who initiates and perfects our faith" (Hebrews 12:2 NLT). God in Christ is not only the Creator and maintainer of our faith, but He is also the sustainer of our daily walk and finisher of our spiritual journey.

Your ordeal is now or soon to be in the past, so there is nothing you can do about it except move forward. Healing is a venture taken with Jesus Himself. Therefore, do not question your future.

After divorce, there are three options—get worse, stay the same, or get better. Moses challenged the Israelites by stating in Deuteronomy 30:19-20 (NLT), "Today I have given you the choice between life and death, between blessings and curses. Now I call on heaven and earth to witness the choice you make. Oh, that you would choose life, so that you and your descendants might live! You can make this choice by loving the Lord your God, obeying him, and committing yourself firmly to him. This is the key to your life. And if you love and obey the Lord, you will live long in the land the Lord swore to give your ancestors Abraham, Isaac, and Jacob." Moses encouraged his fellow Jews to choose life and obey God. God never forces His will upon us. He lets us decide. My prayer for you is to choose life.

People's actions are often controlled by fear and hope. We fear the worst and hope for the best. On a daily basis we should and need to choose life in every situation that arises. Ask yourself, "If I don't choose life, what is the alternative?" The alternative is to live in self-pity, depression, isolation, and resentment your whole life. Do you really want to spend the rest of your life in misery? If you truly want to get better, let go and let God. There is nothing more the devil wants than to see you live in desolation. He wants you feeling completely empty.

Yes, you will never forget your divorce, but do not give it permission to dominate your life. Let it become a learning experience. People have a natural tendency to focus on the negative. I have heard it said, and I strongly agree, it takes more energy to concentrate on the distressing issues of life. All I can simply tell you is to keep fighting. I know you are tired, you're fed up, and you're close to breaking, but there is strength within you—even when you feel weak. Start developing positive beliefs. Discover the dream God has put in your heart. Train yourself to be happy instead of anxious. Good things will come out of bad if you give God the reins. Grow through your pains.

After Stephen was martyred, James wrote to the early Christians to give them hope and encouragement. He said, "Dear brothers and sisters, when troubles of any kind come your way, consider it an opportunity for great joy. For you know that when your faith is tested, your endurance has a chance to grow" (James 1:2-3 NLT). It is not about pretending to be happy when we face pain but having a positive outlook. Tough times can teach us invaluable lessons. Then we really know the depth of our character.

God uses our painful experiences to point us back to Him. Along this journey of rebirth, we begin to understand the depth of God's love for us, His compassion, and the rest that only He can provide. Recovery is not an elusive dream; it is attainable. You know you are there when you stop asking, "When will I know I am healed?" You will realize over time that things will begin to transform as your emotional state becomes manageable. You will not be blaming God or staying angry with Him. Through the process of deepening your relationship with Him, you will begin to create a new normal.

I considered my divorce as a spiritual awakening. It felt as though my life was over. My immediate reflections manifested into feelings of never being happy, being alone the rest of my life, feeling inadequate, and feeling like a total failure. It took me a while to realize it was the devil planting those untruths into my mind. Up to the point of my conversion to a born-again believer in Jesus Christ, I had so many misconceptions of who God really was. I didn't realize how He is really for us and not against us (see Romans 8:31). He definitely has great plans for me and you. I know Jehovah personally mended my broken heart. I discovered joy is truly in the Lord. More importantly, I never felt closer to Him than after my divorce. It is my prayer that you give your life to Christ and you feel humbled by His forgiveness.

As you put God in the center of your life and turn to His spiritual truths, your new perspective on the past will transform the dismal outlook you once had for your future. You begin to see things the way Jesus sees them. You will see your life change. Remember, your past doesn't have the final say. You need to pray, read the Bible daily, and attend a Bible-believing, Bible-teaching church. Start by setting goals for yourself. Do not recast how you handled your previous struggles. Resolve to make wiser responses to what may come up instead of fixing the previous mistakes. Another point that will help you move forward is to stop talking negatively about your former spouse. To do so could be an indicator that you are not fully restored and have not fully forgiven. Realize it is okay to take out the forgiveness book a few times.

David declared in Psalms 31:14-15 (NKJV), "But as for me, I trust in You, O Lord; I say, 'You are my God.' My times are in Your hand; deliver me from the hand of my enemies, and from those who persecute me." In essence, he was saying all of life's circumstances are under God's control—and this was true particularly in his case. David's consciousness of the Lord's presence in his life brought him great comfort. As you begin to fully grasp how much God loves you and cares for you, it will keep you steady in the faith regardless of your circumstances. Think of all the new possibilities ahead of you. The Father of our Lord Jesus Christ will never leave you nor forsake you. You will never be left feeling abandoned. "It is better to take refuge in the Lord than to trust in man" (Psalms 118:8). People will let you down. Only Jesus can get you out of the mire. God's favor enables you to be victorious. Depend upon Him for strength. He brought me solace. Praise God in all His glory because His Son became our salvation.

God knows you personally; He sees your pain. He is not restricted by your current emotional and physical limitations. I have heard people say God will not give you more than you can handle. People get this quote from 1 Corinthians 10:13. This verse deals with handling temptation, not about the hardships and trials of life. The truth is no matter how much the "Great I Am" gives you to bear, even to the point where you concede defeat, He will give you His grace to go through whatever it may be. The Lord declares in Isaiah 43:2-3 (NLT), "When you go through deep waters, I will be with you. When you go through rivers of difficulty, you will not drown. When you walk through the fire of oppression, you will not be burned up; the flames will not consume you. For I am the Lord, your God, the Holy One of Israel, your Savior." Going through difficulty can either cause you to drown or force you to grow stronger. You are more likely to go under if you try to get through it in your own strength. If you invite God to help you, He will protect you.

So my question is, "Do you want to get better?" In John 5, Jesus asked this question to the man who had been disabled for thirty-eight years. He tried to get into the waters at the pool of Bethesda once a year (during Passover) when the waters would be stirred up by an angel and whoever stepped in first was made whole. He told Jesus he had no one to help him into the pool. This was an awkward question to ask, but Jesus wanted to probe the man's desire to be healed. Jesus was moved with compassion by the man's situation. Jesus told him to "Get up! Pick up your mat and walk." The man got up and was healed. He was not healed by his own attempt, but it was through the power of Christ.

When you enter times of trouble or sudden change, you must adjust and keep moving. It is amazing how long people hold on to things that are hurting them. It stills the life God wants us to have. We are afraid to let go of what we know. Life cannot grind to a halt when you experience unpleasant and distressing situations. With the grace of God, keep moving and doing whatever you can rather than giving up because of fear and uncertainty.

No matter the generation, people never change. Each and every person on earth has, at some time, been alone and desperately seeking hope and healing. They usually seek help everywhere else except in Christ. No matter how trapped you feel by your situation, God can minister to your deepest needs. Don't let hardship cause you to lose hope. Jesus not only died on the cross for our sins, but for our needs. He wants us to have faith in Him. I am glad I put my faith and my life in Jesus' hands because the life I have today was a moment-by-moment miracle. You can have it too. Just believe!

Chapter 12

The Free Gift

Chapter 12

The Free Gift

"Jesus answered and said to him, 'Most assuredly, I say to you, unless one is born again, he cannot see the kingdom of God.'"
—John 3:3 NKJV

I was asked the question once, "How can you have faith in someone you can't see?" Well, when you are in a pit of despair feeling hopeless and you have nowhere or no one to turn to and everything you have tried in your own strength has not worked, trying something different seems like a good alternative. Some people keep doing the same thing over and over and get no results. Sometimes it takes a tragic loss to turn to God, but on the other hand some people blame Him and get very angry and question why He allows evil. As a result, they refuse to believe in Him. If God were to prevent all the negative consequences of our actions, would we really have free will? Remember, we live in a sin-fallen world. With a sinful world come evil things.

Regardless if you are a believer or not, do you believe miracles exit? I look around and see miracles everywhere. Not all miracles are huge. Sometimes it's little, everyday miracles that remind me how He is right there beside each and every one of us. I look back from where I was when my life unraveled to now and I know that only God could bring me this far. Don't let tragedy distort your view of God.

Your past should remind you of what God has done for you and encourage you to dedicate or rededicate your life to Him. "Understand, therefore, that the Lord your God is indeed God. He is the faithful God who keeps his covenant for a thousand generations and lavishes his unfailing love on those who love him and obey his commands" (Deuteronomy 7:9 NLT).

God has chosen all believers today to be a part of His treasured family. It is not by any merit of our own that we have come to faith in Christ, but God chose us out of His goodness and grace.

Some of you who have read this book might be Christians already, but some may not. You might remember me mentioning I am a born-again believer in Jesus Christ. You are probably wondering what that means. A born-again Christian is someone who has repented of their sins and has turned to Christ for their salvation, and as a result has become part of God's family forever. We cannot get to heaven based on works, good deeds, or being a good person because by nature we aren't members of God's family. We have been separated from God by sin. The Bible states, "There is none righteous, no, not one" (Romans 3:10 NKJV). And, "For all have sinned and fall short of the glory of God" (Romans 3:23 NKJV).

Due to one man's sin (Adam) we have been separated from God. This resulted in everyone having a sin nature. In God's eyes, even one sin is enough to keep you out of heaven. Consequently, God's plan was to send His Son, Jesus, to die on the cross so we can be reconciled to Him (2 Corinthians 5:18-19). The only thing that can cover our sins is the shed blood of Jesus Christ (Hebrews 9:22). I encourage you, and it is my prayer that you read the prayer below, become part of God's family. You won't regret it; you will see Him do amazing things. "Because, if you confess with your mouth that Jesus is Lord and believe in your heart that God raised him from the dead, you will be saved. For with the heart one believes and is justified, and with the mouth one confesses and is saved" (Romans 10:9-10).

A Suggested Prayer for Salvation:

Heavenly Father, have mercy on me, a sinner. I believe in You and that Your Word is true. I believe that Jesus Christ is the Son of the living God and that He died on the cross so that I may now have forgiveness for my sins and eternal life. I know that without You in my heart, my life is meaningless.

I believe in my heart that You, Lord God, raised Him from the dead. Please, Jesus, forgive me for every sin I have ever committed or done in my heart. Please forgive me and come into my heart as my personal Lord and Savior today. I need You to be my Father and my friend.

I give You my life and ask You to take full control from this moment on. I pray this in the name of Jesus Christ. Amen.

We should be filled with thanksgiving and joy because of what Jesus did on the cross! We have a God who truly understands what we are going through. He has a plan for your life. "For I know the thoughts that I think toward you, says the Lord, thoughts of peace and not of evil, to give you a future and a hope" (Jeremiah 29:11 NKJV).

No matter the struggle, God will see us through to a glorious conclusion!

About the Author

Candy Block was born and raised in Central New York (officially home of the snowiest city in America). In 1992, she received her bachelors of science degree in accounting from King's College. While trying to land her "dream job" in accounting, her aspirations took her on another path. God placed a desire in her heart to write even before her ex-husband left. Since then she's had an article published about lightning in a kid's magazine and is currently working for a large global investment bank. Candy and her husband of over three years, Bob, facilitate Divorce Care at their church to help people heal from the pain of divorce. Candy can be contacted at candith7@gmail.com.

CPSIA information can be obtained
at www.ICGtesting.com
Printed in the USA
FFOW02n1147130317
33350FF